GLASS

TODAY

GLASS
TODAY

American Studio Glass

From Cleveland Collections

Henry H. Hawley

PUBLISHED BY THE CLEVELAND MUSEUM OF ART

Board of Trustees

Contents

Lenders to the Exhibition

JULES AND FRAN BELKIN

MIKE AND ANNIE BELKIN

MR. AND MRS. CHARLES DEBORDEAU

VIRGINIA Q. FOLEY

ANN AND ROBERT FRIEDMAN

ESTER GOLDSMITH

HELEN AND DAVID KANGESSER

RALPH AND TERRY KOVEL

LORRIE AND ALVIN MAGID

ALAN MARKOWITZ, M.D., AND CATHY POLLARD

FRANCINE AND BENSON PILLOFF

CLARINE AND HARVEY SAKS

MR. AND MRS. JAMES A. SAKS

DAN AND LINDA ROCKER SILVERBERG

HEINZ AND ELIZABETH WOLF

PRIVATE COLLECTIONS

THE CLEVELAND MUSEUM OF ART

Glass Today: American Studio Glass from Cleveland Collections celebrates both contemporary glassmaking and the accomplishments of Cleveland area collectors. Drawn from local private collections as well as the museum's holdings, this exhibition provides an overview of trends in the field of glassmaking during the past thirty-five years. Glass Today owes its greatest debt to those ardent collectors who single-mindedly pursued excellence and amazing variety in their purchasing. Now thanks to their largess, the public can share the splendid works they have assembled. Selecting carefully and broadly from their private collections was the task of Henry Hawley, curator of Renaissance and later decorative arts and sculpture. This fine, enticing exhibition is the result of his appreciation of studio glass combined with his meticulous eye for quality. The diversity of the often highly sculptural works attests to the creative possibilities of the medium.

Following last year's bicentennial exhibition initiatives, Transformations in Cleveland Art, 1796–1946 and Urban Evidence: Contemporary Artists Reveal Cleveland, the Cleveland Museum of Art now showcases a number of Cleveland-area glass artists in the context of the national spectrum. Moreover, the exhibition offers an opportunity to display works from private collections alongside pieces from the museum's collection, including many superb gifts that have enlarged its holdings in the contemporary realm. This survey seeks to bring to public attention the technical prowess and artistic power of contemporary American glass artists and the studio glass movement in particular.

We are deeply indebted to Francine Pilloff, who ably led the Exhibition Advisory Committee. Her enthusiasm for glass as a medium for artistic expression is as great as her knowledge of the field. She also chaired the Leadership Gifts Committee, which provided the philanthropic support for both the exhibition and this catalogue. She has been a wonderful resource for the Education Division, helping develop the programming that accompanies the exhibition. In addition, we greatly appreciate her work to promote the exhibition to glass aficionados nationwide. The collecting zeal of Annie and Mike Belkin is well represented in *Glass Today*. Their devotion to glass art matches their support of the museum, to which they have contributed several important works in the past. Others for whom glass is a passion—Fran and Jules Belkin, Mr. and Mrs. Charles Debordeau, Virginia Q. Foley, Ann and Robert Friedman, Ester Goldsmith, Helen and David Kangesser, Terry and Ralph Kovel, Lorrie and Alvin Magid, Cathy Pollard and Alan Markowitz, M.D., Clarine and Harvey Saks, Mr. and Mrs. James A. Saks, Dan and Linda Rocker Silverberg, Elizabeth and Heinz Wolf, and two anonymous lenders—proved to be gracious lenders as well.

The presentation of *Glass Today* was a collaborative effort, spearheaded by Henry Hawley. It involved the creativity of our able chief designer, Jeffrey Strean, the logistical magic of assistant registrar Beth Gresham, and the finesse of packing specialist Andrew Rock. Producing the fine catalogue drew on the expertise of Laurence Channing, head of publications, and Barbara J. Bradley, editor. The often challenging photography work was ably executed by Howard Agriesti, museum photographer. Organizing the myriad details of exhibition production was Katie Solender, exhibition coordinator. Many other departments also deserve thanks for their behind-the-scenes contribution to the successful realization of this project.

For their generosity we gratefully acknowledge the following members of the Glass Today Leadership Gifts Committee: Annie and Mike Belkin, Rosalie and Mort Cohen, Ann and Robert Friedman, Joan Yellen Horvitz, Helen and David Kangesser, Francine and Benson Pilloff, Cathy Pollard and Alan Markowitz, M.D., Cindy and Tom Riley, Dan K. and Linda Rocker Silverberg, two anonymous donors, and the Art Alliance for Contemporary Glass.

Robert P. Bergman, Director

The exhibition *Glass Today: American Studio Glass from Cleveland Collections* has been planned to accomplish several distinct, though related, objectives. First and foremost is to offer the Cleveland public an opportunity to view an assemblage of works summarizing the exciting developments that have occurred in American studio glassmaking of the past three decades. During this period glassmakers, either individuals or small groups of artists, have grown in number from less than a dozen to many hundreds.

By the nature of its manufacture, blown glass tends to assume globular shapes and hence resemble such traditional functional forms for glass as bowls and vases. Although some objects in *Glass Today* recall these vessels, in no case were the works at hand created as useful pieces for normal household service. Instead, they have become sculptures of vessel form. Many, of course, bear no resemblance at all to vessels and can be identified more easily as paintings or sculptures that use glass as at least one of their materials.

The subtitle of the exhibition specifies that pieces are drawn from Cleveland collections, and this aspect constitutes a second objective: to demonstrate the enthusiasm, knowledge, and sensitivity a comparatively small group of local collectors have brought to a specialized but also extremely fertile field of artistic expression. Art collecting seems often to flourish best in circumstances where tastes and interests are shared by several people who can perhaps engage in a sort of cross-fertilization, with the passions of one individual reinforcing those of another even when their points of view may not exactly coincide. Such seems to be the situation prevailing among a number of the collectors who have so generously contributed to this exhibition. Although over the years Cleveland has been the locus of some collections of distinction, this sort of communal encouragement seems a rare phenomenon, encountered here but seldom. The immediate question that arises is "why glass?" At least some answers can be suggested. First among them is the nature of the material itself, its sparkle and brilliant color, its malleability in a molten state that can be adapted to suggest organic forms, and the variety of techniques, and hence results, that can be employed in the creation of a diverse range of works of art. In short, glass affords a wide variety of visual responses, a factor that makes it attractive both to artists who choose it as an expressive medium and to collectors who choose to make it a part of their environments.

A third objective of *Glass Today* is to display the products of glassmaking in this region. Cleveland was the home of one of America's first studio glassmakers, Edris Eckhardt, who was actively producing glass from the 1950s onward; her work is featured in an introductory section of the exhibition. Since the 1970s, glassmaking has been included in the curriculum of the Cleveland Institute of Art; the products of its students and faculty members, especially Brent Kee Young, are represented. Not far from Cleveland, at Kent State University, a pioneer of the American studio glass movement, Henry Halem, has long headed a significant university department for this medium; his work in its considerable variety is represented. Finally, at a greater remove but still within the orbit and thus the consciousness of several Cleveland collectors, was the glassmaking facility Dominick Labino constructed at Grand Rapids, Ohio, not far from Toledo. There he showed the world the technical possibilities available to the studio glass artist.

Despite the important and varied activities of glassmakers in this region, Cleveland did not achieve the significance as a creative center in this medium that the city enjoyed in, for example, ceramic sculpture during the 1930s. Instead, New York and Seattle and, to a lesser extent Providence, Rhode Island, and Penland, North Carolina, as well as the art departments of several midwestern universities, have shared this distinction. Thus, although Cleveland collectors have frequently acquired studio glass made locally, they have often also purchased pieces by artists active outside the area, either directly from their creators or through commercial galleries. Especially important has been the local Riley Hawk Glass Art Galleries, which has done much to interest people of this area in the field of recently made studio glass.

Glass Today demonstrates the variety and richness of local collections of studio glass, but the inclusion of particular examples in the exhibition was a product of my application of the three objectives outlined above. Another different but equally impressive assemblage might have been achieved through the exercise of another person's taste and point of view. Although the focus of the exhibition is on a comparatively brief historical moment (the past thirty years) and most of the pieces included were actually made after 1980, nevertheless the primary objective of this particular occasion—to offer the Cleveland public an opportunity to experience the variety and quality of American studio glass—has meant that several of the outstanding artists in the medium are represented by a group of objects in order to suggest the range of their accomplishment. Because exhibition space is limited, the focus of *Glass Today* is on the work of a comparatively small number of artists whose production seems, from this vantage point in time and on the basis of my personal subjective responses, of compelling interest and merit. Other work by other artists might well have been included, especially that of younger glassmakers who have yet to establish a critical and historical niche for themselves. The work of a few of these artists is on view, but many more might have been discovered, and perhaps they will be included in a future edition of this or a similar exhibition.

G lassmaking is by no means a new technology. The date of its earliest beginnings, probably in Egypt, is difficult to pinpoint exactly, but blown glass used to make vessels was developed in the eastern Mediterranean basin about 2,000 years ago. From a very early time, aesthetic as well as functional motivations inspired the glassmaker, and already under the Romans pieces were sometimes produced in which beauty was clearly the overriding factor in their creation. The Portland Vase at the British Museum is the most famous surviving example of such wares. During the Renaissance decorated glass once again became significant. Venice was the important center of European glassmaking around 1500, and from there styles and techniques for ornamental glass gradually spread through northern Europe (figs. 1–2).

Especially in Germanic central Europe, but also elsewhere on the Continent and even in America beginning in the eighteenth century, there developed a tradition of making functional glass vessels in small isolated rural settings, paralleling other cottage industries of the time (figs. 3–4). In the nineteenth century glassmaking tended to be transferred to larger industrial settings, and gradually the smaller glassmakers disappeared. When, in response to the aesthetic limitations of many industrial products, an effort was made to revive the traditional crafts after the middle of the nineteenth century, glass was generally considered to be technologically too complex a product to be made in the small facilities dedicated to such things as ceramics, furniture making, and metal smithing in the so-called aesthetic mode and a bit later, toward 1900, in the Arts and Crafts style. Glassmaking related stylistically to the more advanced taste of the late nineteenth and early twentieth centuries was generally accomplished in factories headed by designers of talent who determined the nature of their product but did not themselves make it.

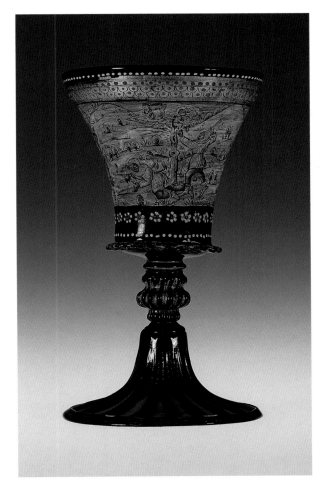

Fig. 1. Italy, Venice. *The Pedlar Goblet*, about 1475. Green and turquoise glass, enameled and gilded, h. 21.4 (8⁷⁄₁₆). Purchase from the J. H. Wade Fund 1953.364.

Fig. 2. Germany, Thuringia. *Flute*, early 17th century. Glass, h. 33.0 (13). John L. Severance Fund 1951.545.

Fig. 3. Germany, probably Saxony. *Beaker*, dated 1653. Green glass ("Waldglas") with prunts, h. 12.5 (4¹⁵⁄₁₆). Purchase from the J. H. Wade Fund 1991.19.

Fig. 4. United States, South Jersey. *Sugar Bowl*, about 1840. Blue glass, h. 14.0 (5½). John L. Severance Fund 1951.110.

Fig. 5. Emile Gallé (French, 1846–1904). *Vase,* about 1900. Glass, cameo cut with pink and green inclusions, h. 13.5 (5⁵⁄₁₆). Andrew R. and Martha Holden Jennings Fund 1979.10.

Fig. 7. Louis Comfort Tiffany (American, 1848–1933). *Vase,* about 1919. Glass, h. 19.4 (7⅝). Norman O. Stone and Ella A. Stone Memorial Fund 1970.126.

Fig. 6. Firm of René Lalique (French, 1860–1945). *Vase,* about 1930. Pale blue gray opalescent glass, h. 25.4 (10). Gift of Mrs. Arthur L. Brockway 1963.247.

Fig. 8. Designed by Viktor Emanuel Lindstrand (Swedish, 1904–1983), made by AB Orrefors Glasbruk. *Zebra Vase,* 1939. Glass, h. 23.0 (9⅛). Dudley P. Allen Fund 1939.676.

Fig. 9. Designed by Sidney Waugh (American, 1904–1963), made at Steuben Glass, Inc., Corning, New York. *Bowl: Europa,* 1935. Glass, h. 24.3 (9⁹⁄₁₆). Dudley P. Allen Fund 1938.381.

Emile Gallé and René Lalique in France and Louis Comfort Tiffany in the United States are perhaps the best known of such heads of glass firms (figs. 5–7), but a number of other European and American counterparts can be identified. It became an almost universally held assumption that glass, especially blown glass, could only be made successfully in a factorylike setting where teams of highly skilled workers could be assembled to execute the basic forms and where the materials needed were provided in relatively large quantities—factors thought to assure quality. Thus, until after the middle of the twentieth century, virtually all the glass aspiring to aesthetic excellence produced in Europe and America was made in factories, at first largely in those owned and operated by designers of distinction. Later, in establishments of a more fundamentally commercial nature, designers were employed to gain for their firms a reputation for aesthetic excellence and thus promote their general economic well-being. From the 1920s onward a number of instances of this kind can be cited, among them the Orrefors firm in Sweden and Steuben in America (figs. 8–9). During the post–World War II era, when Czechoslovakia was ruled by a Communist government, it became customary in nationalized glass factories to supply facilities for artists to work on independent projects only marginally related to the functional products that were the factories' chief commodity. Under these circumstances some of the most adventuresome and aesthetically significant glass of the time was realized.

The distinction that defines studio glassmaking and sets it apart from factory work is that it is based upon the efforts of a single individual or a small group of persons who both determine the design of their products and accomplish the technical and craft processes necessary for their execution. It is further presumed that their artistic ambitions will be more complex and sophisticated than those of the small commercial glass houses that had existed into the nineteenth century. In some instances it can be difficult to distinguish between studio glassmaking and that produced in a small factory, but following the definition outlined here, the former seems to have emerged in France in the late nineteenth century. The first studio glassmaker was probably Henri Cros (p. 20), who was trained as both a painter and a sculptor and was interested in amalgamating the two media. First he worked with colored wax and then, in the early 1880s, began trying to revive an ancient technique of mixing ground glass with pigments, placing the resulting paste in a mold, and heating it until the glass melted enough to fuse. Although simple in principle, this medium, called *pâte-de-verre*, proved difficult in practice because of the problem of controlling the colors when heated. By the end of the decade Cros had achieved a degree of success, and in 1890 he received an appointment at the official French porcelain factory at Sèvres, on the outskirts of Paris, which allowed him access to its facilities, especially large kilns in which he could fire monumental works in pâte-de-verre. The material achieved a measure of popularity and was imitated by other artists, among them François-Émile Décorchement (p. 21), who succeeded Cros at Sèvres after the latter's death in 1907.

In the 1920s another Frenchman, Maurice Marinot (pp. 21–2), made an even bolder step. Trained as a painter, he exhibited with the Fauves in 1905 but in 1911 became intrigued with glass. At first he decorated glass with enamel, but having learned to blow glass, from 1920 onward he produced unique objects in this fashion, becoming the first fully trained artist to practice the craft instead of relying on others to execute his designs. Marinot's artistic and technical accomplishment resulted in some much-admired glass objects that, though of vessel forms, were clearly intended not for functional purposes but for aesthetic contemplation, that is, essentially as small sculptures in a very broad connotation of that term. Marinot had some direct followers in France, among them Henri Navarre (p. 22).

Marinot's work was not well known in America until after 1960, but artists interested in making glass knew of him, and, even though they did not follow directly in his stylistic and technological footsteps, he existed as a possible role model in the depths of their consciousness. The beginnings of studio glassmaking in America, however, are to be found among artists who crafted glass by means other than blowing. At first the most important of these alternative techniques were slumping and fusing. Sheets of glass of a predetermined size were put in a kiln, sometimes on top of a form or mold, and then heated. Just before reaching its melting point, the glass would sag, filling a mold or dropping over the sides of a form and creating a shallow vessel. Colored enamels and small bits of metal could be fused into the surface of the glass for ornamental purposes, or sheets of glass, sometimes previously decorated, could be laminated together by fusing them. Maurice Heaton is the best-known glass artist working in this slump technique in the 1940s and 1950s, and Earl McCutchen (p. 26) also used this method, relying on commercially produced glass for his raw product. During the same time, other artist-craftsmen such as Frederick Carder and Harvey K. Littleton (pp. 29–31) made cast glass sculptures and vessels, but only occasionally. In the 1950s in Cleveland, Edris Eckhardt (pp. 23–5) first made translucent glass plaques by joining together sheets of glass decorated with gold leaf and enamels; at a slightly later time, into the 1960s, she made cast glass sculptures, sometimes combining metal with glass.

A third alternative method of glassmaking existed but was seldom employed in the United States by serious artist-craftsmen. Called lamp work, it is essentially glassblowing but on a very small scale, using an open flame to heat the material while it is manipulated. The small glass figures and animals traditionally produced at fairs and carnivals are examples of lamp work at its most primitive, and the blown glass ornaments within glass paperweights are also made in this fashion and then embedded in clear glass. In Germany the lamp work technique has been used to produce small but sophisticated vessel forms, but nothing comparable has been made in the United States.

By the early 1960s it was clear that a number of American artist-craftsmen, often trained as ceramists, were becoming interested in glass as a medium of aesthetic expression. The year 1962 was the *annus mirabilis* of studio glassmaking in the United States and later, by extension, throughout the world. Harvey Littleton, a professor of ceramics at the University of Wisconsin, had long been associated with glassmaking through his father, who was director of research at the Corning Glass Works. From 1949 to 1951 Littleton had worked as a ceramics instructor at the Toledo Museum of Art and become acquainted with Dominick Labino (pp. 26–9), vice president and director of research at Johns-Manville Fiber Glass Corporation, who took evening craft classes at the museum. After a European trip devoted to observing glassmaking, Littleton attempted some experiments with the medium in 1958 and reported on them at a conference of the American Craftsmen's Council in 1959. For several years Littleton pursued his interest in glass and gradually inspired the interest of other colleagues. He persuaded Otto Wittmann, then director of the Toledo Museum of Art, to sponsor a glassblowing workshop at the museum from 23 March to 1 April 1962. Among those participating was Labino, who offered valuable technical knowledge to the largely inexperienced participants. Harvey Leafgreen, a retired blower from Libbey Glass, demonstrated blowing techniques. Littleton's enthusiasm and the knowledge and experience of Labino and Leafgreen proved a happy mix, and the workshop produced unexpected progress. The success of the first workshop resulted in an even more ambitious one held in June of the same year, and on the basis of these events, the studio glass movement in the United States was launched. In the fall of 1962 Littleton began organizing a department for glassmaking at the University of Wisconsin, Madison, and soon thereafter its graduates went forth to establish university-allied and other centers for glass artists literally from coast to coast. In 1965 Labino took early retirement and began to devote himself to his own glassblowing and to supplying others with the knowledge and materials necessary to pursue their ambitions in the field.

In the wake of Littleton and Labino followed a group of glassmakers, some of whom were their students or recipients of their knowledge and influence. Others seem to have operated almost entirely independently. Several of these pioneers of American studio glass are represented in this exhibition, often by examples recently created. Marvin Lipofsky (p. 40) studied under Littleton at the University of Wisconsin and then went on to the Bay Area to teach and practice his art of hot glassblowing, while Henry Halem (pp. 36–8) came to Kent State University but soon gave up blowing for glass panels. Another champion of the hot blown glass technique, Dale Chihuly (pp. 40–51), was also at Wisconsin in the mid-1960s and then carried his imaginative inventions in glassmaking first to the Rhode Island School of Design in Providence, and a bit later, in the 1970s, to the Pilchuck Glass School near Seattle. Through those two institutions have passed some of the best-known contemporary glassmakers, for example, Howard Ben Tré (pp. 78–80), Dan Dailey (pp. 62–3), Michael M. Glancy (p. 89), and Steven Weinberg (pp. 81–2). More recently, a number of artists associated with Chihuly at Pilchuck have emerged as significant practitioners in their own right, among them Flora C. Mace and Joey Kirkpatrick (pp. 100–2) and William Morris (pp. 108–11), and the Seattle region has become perhaps the single most important center of American studio glassmaking. The careers of contemporary glass artists are often peripatetic, and two whose activities have been centered in New York City are John Brekke (p. 72) and Steve Tobin (p. 108).

A number of important glass artists have long been associated with the Penland School of Crafts where Labino aided with the initial installation of equipment for the glass department. Mark Peiser (pp. 33–4) and Richard Q. Ritter Jr. (p. 39) have consistently demonstrated a focus on technical excellence that is part of the Labino legacy. Still others have found career paths outside the customary ones outlined here. Joel Philip Myers (pp. 31–2) came to glass-making through training in graphic and industrial design. Paul Stankard's (pp. 51–5) earliest training was in scientific glassblowing. Michael Pavlik (p. 65–6), who was born in Prague, enjoyed the benefits of a Czech education as a glass artist before coming to the United States. Still others, such as Brent Kee Young (pp. 57–8), stand apart in terms of their training. It is clear that though the beginnings of the studio glass movement in America can be plotted, much variety existed and continues to exist today in the way people have been trained and the styles and techniques they choose to pursue in their mature work.

In preparing this exhibition, I suddenly became aware that a very large proportion of the exhibitors had been born within a few years of 1950, meaning that many of them were receiving their training about 1970, a time when the studio glass movement was in full swing. Although hot glassblowing continued to be the dominant technique of those in the field, other possibilities for the fabrication and decoration of glass were beginning to open up. Casting, slumping, and laminating were alternatives used by some, and enamel paint, sandblasting, and cutting and polishing are only a sampling of the modes of decoration available. A sumptuous banquet of technical choices was presented and used to make a wide range of two- and three-dimensional objects in which glass was an important, but often not the only, material.

Studio glassmaking continues to be an active field, but what courses will be followed by the generation following that of 1950 remains as yet undefined. Perhaps innovations will be ones of expression rather than of technical resources, but only when a large body of aesthetically significant work has been realized and recognized will the future of studio glass become fully apparent.

H. H. H.

Catalogue

Henri Cros

Incantation, 1892
Pâte-de-verre; 33.4 x 23.3
(13⅛ x 9⅛)
The Cleveland Museum of
Art, James Parmelee Fund
1969.24

Born in Narbonne, France, Cros (1840–1907) began his studies at thirteen in the Paris studio of genre painter Jules Valadon. Impressed by a bas-relief, Valadon encouraged Cros to continue his efforts in sculpture, which then led him to study with the academic sculptor Antoine Etex. Around 1870 Cros began to develop an interest in the nearly lost ancient medium of encaustic painting, in which pigment is blended and applied in hot wax. This pursuit probably led to experiments in colored wax reliefs that, in turn, led to his rediscovery of another neglected ancient technique—*pâte-de-verre.* In this medium ceramists' pigments are blended with powdered glass and fused in a kiln. In 1890 Cros was appointed to a post at the Sèvres porcelain factory, where he was able to expand the scale of his works in pâte-de-verre.

François-Émile Décorchemont

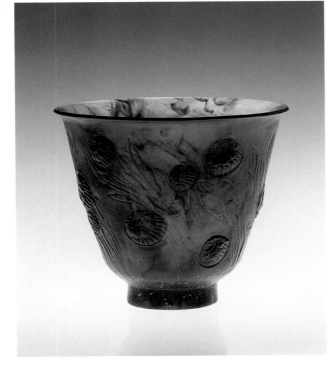

Vase, about 1922
Pâte-de-verre; h. 10
(3¹⁵⁄₁₆), diam. 11.6 (4⁹⁄₁₆)
The Cleveland Museum
of Art, Gift of Louise
Rorimer Dushkin
1983.210

Décorchemont (1880–1971) graduated from the École Nationale des Arts Décoratifs in Paris in 1900. From 1901 to 1903 he began to work in ceramics but was soon discouraged by difficulties with the stoneware clay body he used, especially with the high firing temperatures it required. At his father's encouragement, he decided to try glass media, including pâte-de-verre, and in 1903 exhibited a well-received leaded-glass piece in the Salon des Artistes. Around 1907–8 he started to introduce powdered lead-crystal glass into the body of his pâte-de-verre, which increased its translucency. Soon after, he returned to his native Conches and conducted experiments using colored powdered-crystal glass as his base, molding it in the lost-wax technique normally associated with metalworking. In the 1930s Décorchemont made critically acclaimed leaded-glass windows in which each piece of glass was made by this method.

Maurice Marinot

Blue-Green Bottle, about 1924–25
Blown glass, acid etched;
16.8 x 10.4 (6⁹⁄₁₆ x 4¹⁄₁₆)
The Cleveland Museum of
Art, Dudley P. Allen Fund
1938.382

Although Marinot (1882–1960) enrolled in the École des Beaux-Arts in 1901, he received most of his education outside the classroom. He exhibited with his former classmate André Derain and others in the ground-breaking Salon d'Automne of 1905, where they earned the name Les Fauves. His interest in glassmaking started upon visiting the Viard glassworks in 1911; he began by designing pieces to be executed there. However, his growing interest in the qualities of glass led him to learn glassblowing from his friends the Viard brothers. Marinot began to experiment with impure glass usually rejected for its bubbly consistency. Later he colored the glass with metallic oxides blown between layers and etched thick forms with repeated acid baths. His innovative style was well received in the 1920s and would later influence others, especially in France.

Vase, 1928
Blown glass, acid etched; h. 22 (8⅝), diam. 16.6 (6½)
The Cleveland Museum of Art, Gift of C. M. de Hauke 1929.114

Henri Navarre

Vase, about 1930–35
Blown glass; h. 22.5 (8¹³⁄₁₆), diam. 14.6 (5¾)
The Cleveland Museum of Art, The A. W. Ellenberger Sr. Endowment Fund 1977.12

Navarre (1885–1971) entered the École Bernard Palissy in 1903 to study sculpture. He was then apprenticed to a silversmith before studying mosaic and leaded glass-making at the Conservatoire National des Arts et Métiers in Paris. In 1924 his interest in glassmaking was confirmed after designing a leaded-glass window for the offices of the paper *l'Intransigeant.* His use of massive, roughly etched glass in several windows indicates strongly the influence of Maurice Marinot, as do many of Navarre's later pieces of blown glass.

Edris Eckhardt

Cherubim, 1955
Cast glass; 15 x 22.1 (5⅞ x
8¹¹⁄₁₆)
The Cleveland Museum of
Art, Gift of The Cleveland
Art Association 1956.92

Cleveland native Eckhardt (1907–) had enjoyed a long,
successful career as a ceramist when in 1953 she began
experiments in glassmaking. At first she made laminated
glass panels decorated with gold leaf and enamels; she
later turned to sculpture made of cast glass, sometimes
combined with metal.

Untitled, 1969
Cast glass; 31 x 21.2 (12³⁄₁₆
x 8⁵⁄₁₆)
Ralph and Terry Kovel
Collection

Horse, 1976
Cast glass; 20 x 13.8 x 8.1
(7⅞ x 5½ x 3¼)
The Cleveland Museum of
Art, Gift of Mr. and Mrs.
Samuel H. Lamport
1994.217

*In the Garden of the Sea
(Neither Night Nor Day),*
1979
Laminated glass; 29.5 x
10.7 (11⅝ x 4¼)
Heinz and Elizabeth Wolf
Collection

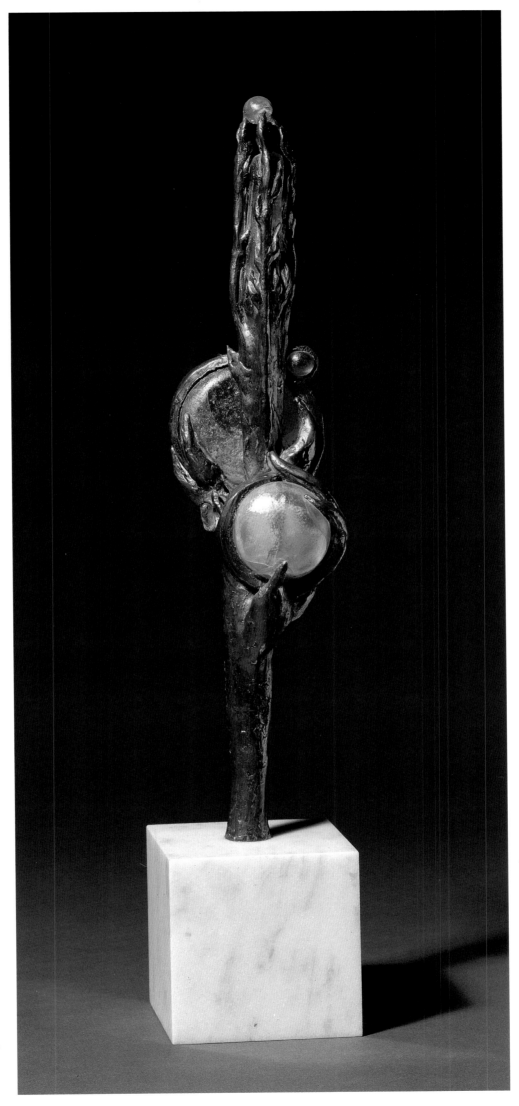

Wonder, 1982
Cast bronze and glass; h.
41.5 (16⁵⁄₁₆), with base 52.4
x 9 (20⅝ x 3½)
Heinz and Elizabeth Wolf
Collection

Earl McCutchen

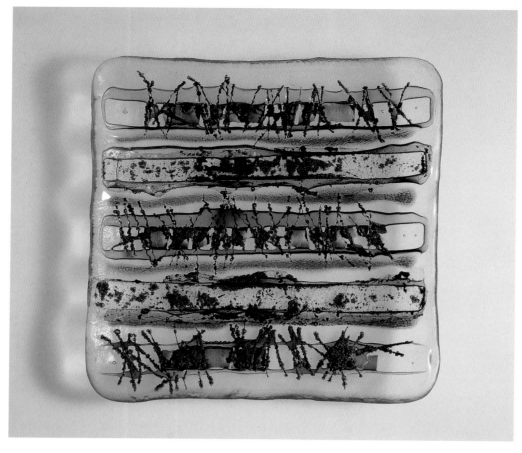

Plate, 1960
Slumped glass; 1.4 x 17.2
x 17.2 (½ x 6¾ x 6¾)
The Cleveland Museum of
Art, Anonymous Gift
1960.263

A ceramist by training, McCutchen (1918–1985) taught for many years in the art department of the University of Georgia. Rather late in his career he began experimenting with glass, especially with laminating and slumping sheets of glass and decorating them with enamels and metal inclusions.

Dominick Labino

Iceberg, 1965
Blown glass; h. 21.6 (8½)
The Cleveland Museum of
Art, Gift of the artist
1967.161

Labino (1910–1987) had an extended, highly successful career as scientist and engineer. He was vice president and director of research at the Johns-Manville Fiber Glass Corporation. In the 1950s Labino participated in evening craft classes at the Toledo Museum of Art School of Design and at that time met Harvey Littleton. When the Toledo workshops were organized in 1962, Labino contributed his technical expertise and suggested to Littleton and others materials and equipment that made studio glassmaking possible. In 1965 Labino took early retirement and set up his own glassmaking establishment in Grand Rapids, Ohio, near Toledo. He continued to share his knowledge of glass technology with many American glass artists.

Vase, 1965
Blown glass; 25.8 x 16.8
(10⅛ x 6¹¹⁄₁₆)
The Cleveland Museum of
Art, Gift of the artist
1967.162

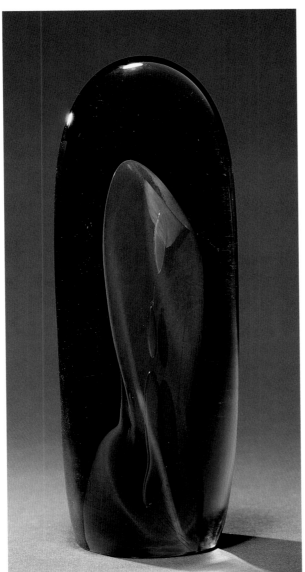

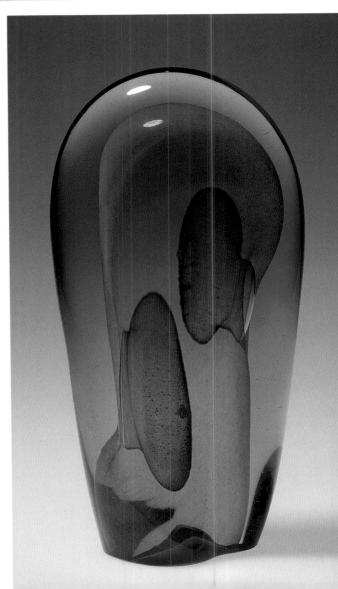

Emergence, 1969
Blown glass; 26.1 x 9.7 x 8
(10¼ x 3¹³⁄₁₆ x 3³⁄₁₆)
The Cleveland Museum of
Art, Gift of Mr. and Mrs.
Samuel H. Lamport
1994.215

Untitled, 1970
Blown glass; 26 x 13.3
(10³⁄₁₆ x 5³⁄₁₆)
Collection of Mr. and Mrs.
James A. Saks

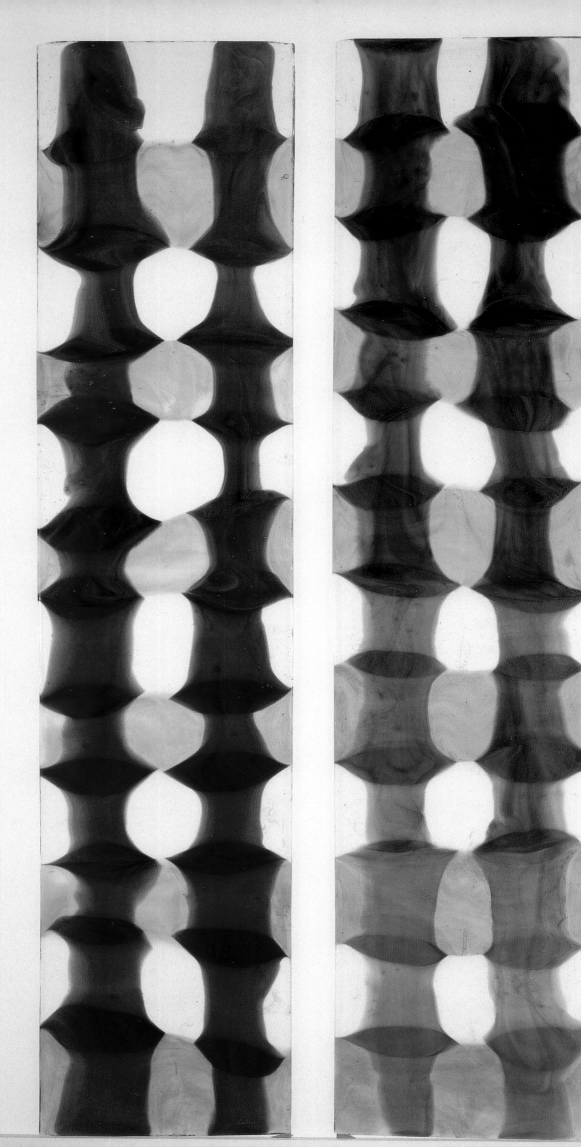

Long-Chain Molecules, 1973
Cast glass; 200.6 x 45.7 x
1.8 (79 x 18 x $^{11}/_{16}$), 201.4 x
45.7 x 1.9 (79$^5/_{16}$ x 18 x ¾)
The Cleveland Museum of
Art, Gift of Carol and
Franklin Milgrim in honor
of Berenice Kent 1991.31,
1991.32

Faceted Fountain, 1978
Blown glass; 17.2 x 14.3 x
9.7 (6¾ x 5⅝ x 3¹³⁄₁₆)
The Cleveland Museum of
Art, Gift of Mr. and Mrs.
James A. Saks 1980.124

Harvey K. Littleton

Descending Sliced Arches,
1984
Blown glass; part 1: 20.4 x
15.3 x 5.2 (8 x 6 x 2), part
2: 38.2 x 15.3 x 28 (15 x 6
x 11), part 3: 38.2 x 15.3 x
28 (15 x 6 x 11), part 4:
20.4 x 15.3 x 5.2 (8 x 6 x 2)
Collection of Alan
Markowitz, M.D., and
Cathy Pollard

Littleton (1922–) is perhaps the single most important figure in the American studio glass movement. Because his father was director of research for Corning Glass Works, from an early age he had access to glassmaking activities. From 1949 to 1951 Littleton was a ceramics instructor at the Toledo Museum of Art School of Design where he met Dominick Labino, who was destined to supply much of the technical knowledge for early studio glassmakers. In the latter year Littleton earned an M.F.A. in ceramics at Cranbrook Academy of Art near Detroit and began teaching at the University of Wiscon-

sin, Madison. Littleton's interest in glass persisted, but it was not until the Toledo workshops of 1962 that studio glassmaking became more than experimentation for him. Shortly thereafter he established a glassmaking program at Madison in which many future artists in the medium participated. He also became a major artist working with glass.

Purple Conical Intersection,
1985
Blown glass; 24.2 x 24.1
(9½ x 9⁷⁄₁₆)
Helen and David
Kangesser Collection

Descending Arch, 1988
Blown glass; part 1: 16.7 x
11.3 (6⁹⁄₁₆ x 4⁷⁄₁₆), part 2:
36.8 x 25.9 (14⁷⁄₁₆ x 10³⁄₁₆)
Clarine and Harvey Saks
Collection

Standing Mobile Arc, 1989
Blown glass; part 1: 12.5 x
12.9 (4⅞ x 5¹⁄₁₆), part 2:
49.1 x 38.2 (19⁵⁄₁₆ x 15)
Lorrie and Alvin Magid
Collection

Joel Philip Myers

Contiguous Fragment Series,
1981
Blown glass, acid etched,
and applied glass elements;
31.8 x 11.2 (12½ x 4⅜)
Mike and Annie Belkin
Collection

After working as a graphic and industrial designer in the
1950s, Myers (1934–) graduated from Alfred University
in New York in 1963 with a degree in ceramics. He had
some exposure to glassblowing at Alfred. The year he
graduated he went to work for the Blenko Glass
Company in West Virginia, where he was allowed to
experiment with glass and eventually became a skilled
glassblower. In 1970 he established a program in glass at
Illinois State University.

Arctic Landscape II, 1990
Blown glass; 38.2 x 45 (15
x 17¹¹⁄₁₆)
Private collection

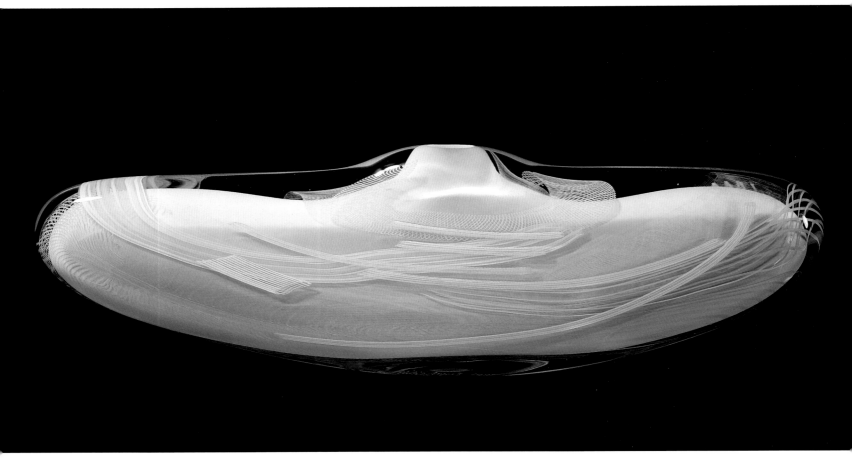

Arctic Sky II, 1991
Blown glass; 22.2 x 73.8
(8¾ x 29¹⁄₁₆)
Helen and David
Kangesser Collection

Mark Peiser

Leaning Moon, 1985
Cast glass, cut and pol-
ished; 23.3 x 20 (9⅛ x 7⅞)
Helen and David
Kangesser Collection

Peiser (1938–) has long been associated with the Penland
School of Crafts in North Carolina, where in 1967 he
was the first hot glass artist-in-residence. In recent times
he has turned to cast, cut, and polished glass sculptures of
subtle design and color.

Ascension Series, 1986
Cast glass, cut and pol-
ished; 35.6 x 17.2 x 7.6
(14 x 6¾ x 3)
Mike and Annie Belkin
Collection

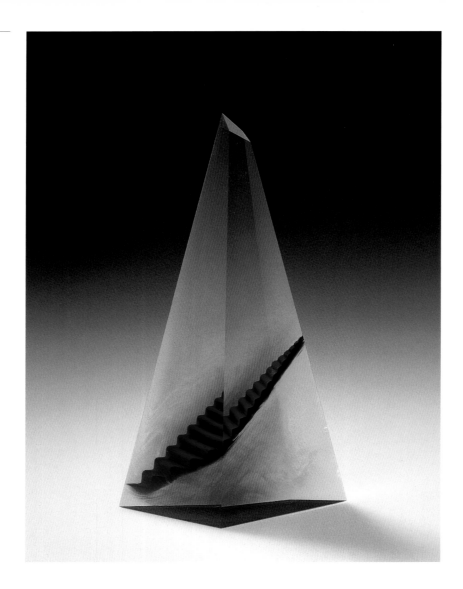

Escher's Tower, 1986
Cast glass, cut and pol-
ished; 35.9 x 20 (14⅛ x
7⅞)
Mike and Annie Belkin
Collection

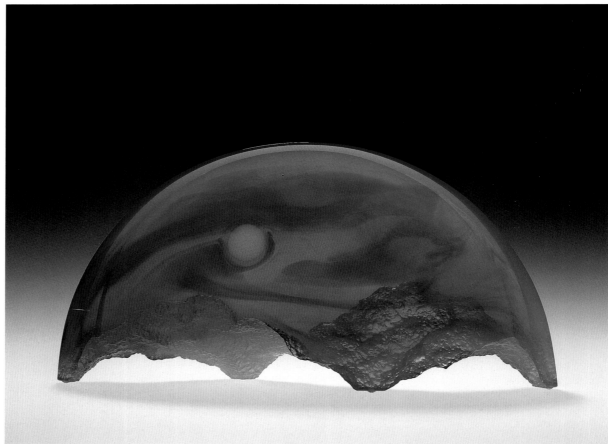

Mountain Skyscape, 1993
Cast glass, cut and pol-
ished; 21.5 x 43.1 (8⁷⁄₁₆ x
16¹⁵⁄₁₆)
Ann and Robert Friedman
Collection

Italo Scanga

Endangered Species Series: Spotted Owl, 1993
Blown glass and painted metal; 87 x 30.9 (34¼ x 12⅛)
Ann and Robert Friedman Collection

Of Italian birth, Scanga (1932–) graduated from Michigan State University and has taught at the University of California, San Diego. Glass has long been one of his technical resources, but he customarily makes use of other materials as well in the creation of his sculptures.

Henry Halem

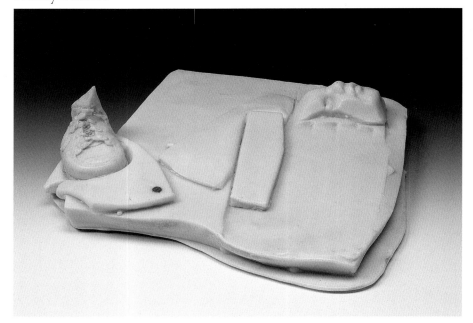

Baby Doll, 1976
Cast glass; 31.1 x 33.4 x
8.3 (12¼ x 13⅛ x 3¼)
Mike and Annie Belkin
Collection

Halem (1938–) has headed the glass studies department at
Kent State University since 1969. He trained at, among
other places, the Rhode Island School of Design. Over
the years he has made a wide variety of glass vessels and
sculpture, but more recently he has focused on low-relief
wall panels with painting and other decorations.

Bowl, 1977
Blown glass; h. 14.7 (5¾),
diam. 15.9 (6¼)
The Cleveland Museum of
Art, Gift of Mr. and Mrs.
Samuel H. Lamport
1994.214

Black Nude, 1984
Vitrolite with painted
enamel; 61 x 61 (24 x 24)
Mike and Annie Belkin
Collection

Constructivist Construction,
1986
Glass (with plastic?); 104.6
x 80.5 (41³⁄₁₆ x 31¹¹⁄₁₆)
Heinz and Elizabeth Wolf
Collection

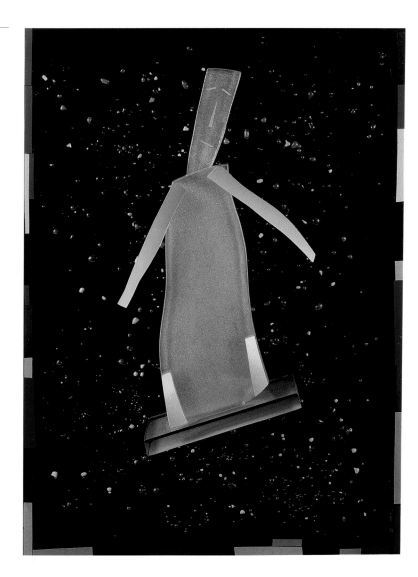

Figure #1, 1988
Vitrolite with painted
enamel; 64.8 x 48.3 x 8.9
(25½ x 19 x 3½)
Mike and Annie Belkin
Collection

Fritz Dreisbach

Vase, 1986
Blown glass; 24.4 x 19.7
(9⁹⁄₁₆ x 7¾)
Mike and Annie Belkin
Collection

A native of Cleveland, Dreisbach (1941–) attended Hiram College and Oberlin. Later he received an M.F.A. from the University of Wisconsin, Madison. He works primarily with hot blown glass. In recent years he has been closely associated with Seattle glassmaking and the nearby Pilchuck Glass School.

Richard Q. Ritter Jr.

Bowl, 1975
Blown glass; h. 15 (5⅞),
diam. 16.4 (6½)
The Cleveland Museum of
Art, Gift of Mr. and Mrs.
Samuel H. Lamport
1994.216

Born in Detroit, Ritter (1940–) has been associated with
the Penland School of Crafts for most of his life. His
glassmaking is particularly identified with blown glass
vessels incorporating as at least part of their decoration
slices from canes of glass he makes for that purpose.

Large Bowl, 1994
Blown glass with inclu-
sions; h. 13.2 (5³⁄₁₆), diam.
30.6 (12)
Ann and Robert Friedman
Collection

Marvin Lipofsky

*California Color Series
1986−87 #16,* 1986−87
Blown glass; 27.3 x 34.2
(10¾ x 13⁷⁄₁₆)
Clarine and Harvey Saks
Collection

Lipofsky (1938−) had already obtained a degree in industrial design when, in 1964, he became one of Littleton's first students of glassmaking at the University of Wisconsin. That same year Lipofsky began a teaching career in the Bay Area, at the University of California, Berkeley, and the California College of Arts and Crafts. Unlike many of his contemporaries, Lipofsky has maintained his early interest in hot blown glass, and using that medium, he has produced abstract glass sculpture of rounded organic forms.

Dale Chihuly

Blanket Series, Untitled,
1976
Blown glass; 29 x 18.7
(11³⁄₈ x 7⁵⁄₁₆)
Heinz and Elizabeth Wolf
Collection

Blanket Series, Untitled,
1976
Blown glass; 27.9 x 14.3
(11 x 5⅝)
Heinz and Elizabeth Wolf
Collection

After studying with Littleton at the University of Wisconsin in 1966, Chihuly (1941–) moved on to the Rhode Island School of Design where he received his M.F.A. in 1968. In that year he received a Fulbright Scholarship to refine his skills as a glassblower by working at the Venini factory in Venice. In the 1970s Chihuly began to explore the possibilities of glass sculptures and developed surface decoration techniques. That decade also saw the formation of Pilchuck, the school and glassmaking center near Seattle with which Chihuly has long been associated. The loss of an eye put an end to Chihuly's personal activities as a glassblower, but he has continued to head a very productive group of glassmakers.

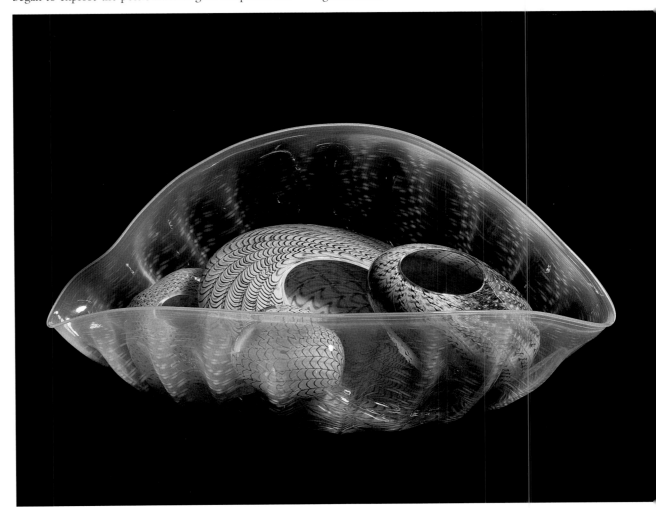

Early White Seaform Set,
1981
Blown glass; 18.2 x 47.3
(7⅛ x 18⅝)
Francine and Benson
Pilloff Collection

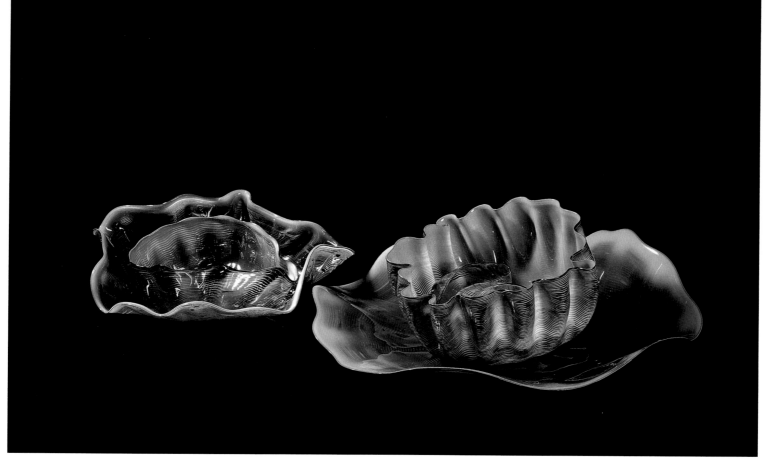

*Gray Seaform Macchia Set
with Black Lip Wrap,* 1983
Blown glass; 16.7 x 51.1
(6⁹⁄₁₆ x 20⅛)
Francine and Benson
Pilloff Collection

Lavender Persian Set, 1988
Blown glass; 21 x 57.5 (8¼
x 22⅝)
Lorrie and Alvin Magid
Collection

■ 42

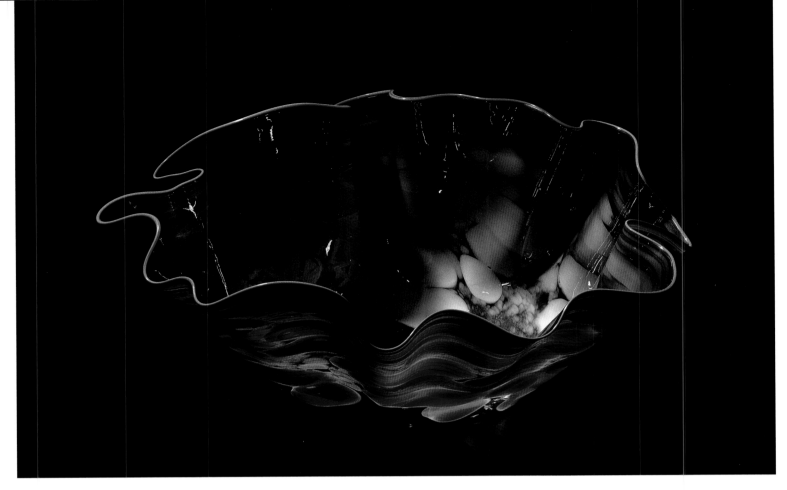

Macchia, 1988
Blown glass; 41.6 x 81.8
(16⅜ x 32³⁄₁₆)
Francine and Benson
Pilloff Collection

Cadmium Yellow Persian Set, 1990
Blown glass; 21.9 x 47.9 x 24.4 (8⅝ x 18¹³⁄₁₆ x 9⁹⁄₁₆)
The Cleveland Museum of Art, The Mary Spedding
Milliken Memorial Collection, Gift of William
Mathewson Milliken 1991.76

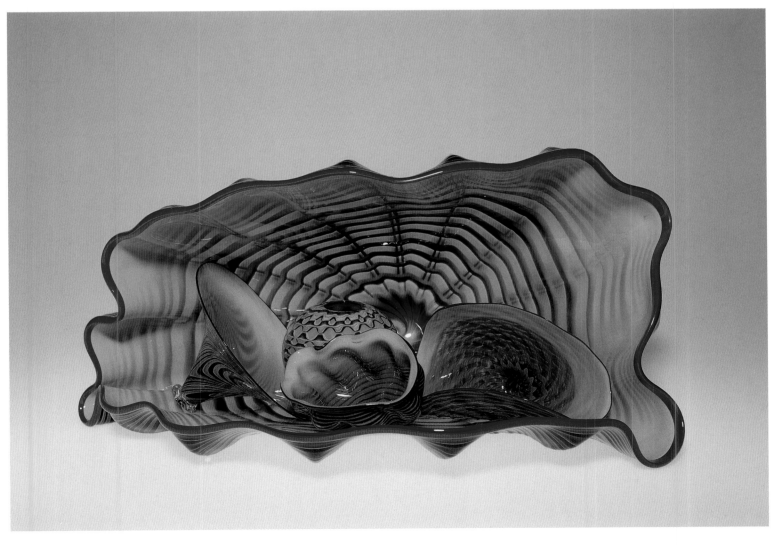

*Cobalt Green and Violet
Wall Piece,* 1990
Blown glass; 91.4 x 152.4
x 45.8 (36 x 60 x 18)
Collection of Alan
Markowitz, M.D., and
Cathy Pollard

*Gilded Yellow Venetian with
Lilies,* 1991
Blown glass; 52.5 x 57
(20⅝ x 22⁷⁄₁₆)
Francine and Benson
Pilloff Collection

*Gold over Cobalt Blue
Venetian with One Coil,*
1991
Blown glass; 78.4 x 33
(30⅞ x 13)
Francine and Benson
Pilloff Collection

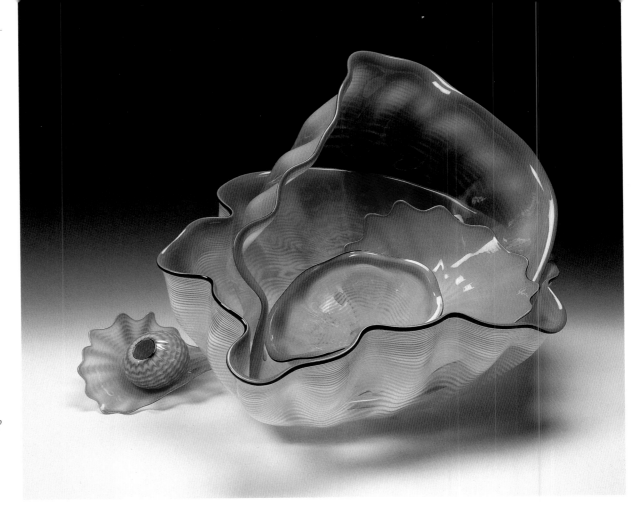

*Pink Seaform with Black Lip
Wraps,* 1991
Blown glass; 34.3 x 53.3
x 45.7 (13½ x 21 x 18)
Mike and Annie Belkin
Collection

*Gilded Blue Tortoise Shell
Float,* 1992
Blown glass; 57.1 x 66.5
(22½ x 26³⁄₁₆)
Francine and Benson
Pilloff Collection

*Green and Oxblood Ikebana
with Two Red Flowers,* 1992
Blown glass; 154.9 x 99 x
43.2 (61 x 39 x 17)
Francine and Benson
Pilloff Collection

*Silver over Rose Madder
Drawing Float*, 1992
Blown glass; 55.9 x 45.8
x 55.9 (22 x 18 x 22)
Collection of Mr. and Mrs.
Charles Debordeau

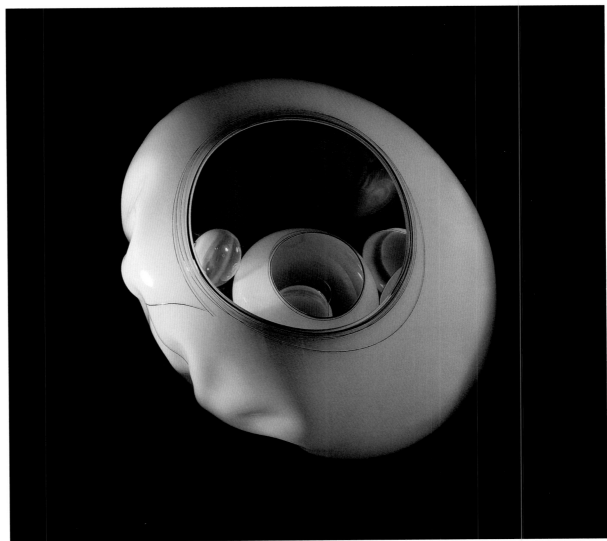

*Translucent White Basket Set
with Black Lip Wraps*, 1992
Blown glass; 45.2 x 57.2
(17¾ x 22½)
Francine and Benson
Pilloff Collection

Green and Magenta Chandelier,
1995
Blown glass; 61 x 76.2 x 76.2
(24 x 30 x 30)
Francine and Benson Pilloff
Collection

Periwinkle Blue Macchia with Black Lip Wrap, 1995
Blown glass; 29 x 40.5
(11⅜ x 15¹⁵⁄₁₆)
Dan and Linda Rocker
Silverberg Collection

Paul J. Stankard

Water Lily Environment with Spirits, 1987
Lamp-worked and encased glass; h. 5 (1¹⁵⁄₁₆), diam. 8.4 (3¼)
Virginia Q. Foley
Collection

Trained as a scientific glassblower, Stankard (1943–) employs the comparatively rare technique of lamp work to create the flowers and animals used as the central motifs in his small sculptures. He has developed an extraordinary dexterity in the production of realistic subjects that he sometimes combines with tiny representations of nude figures. He is widely recognized for his technical accomplishment in his chosen mode of work. Rick Ayotte (1944–), a maker of paperweights who resides in New Hampshire, made the turtle Stankard incorporated into *Environmental with Turtle.*

Allium, 1989
Lamp-worked and encased
glass; 12.7 x 7.3 x 7 (5 x
2⅞ x 2¾)
The Cleveland Museum of
Art, Seventy-fifth anniver-
sary gift of the George M.
Foley Family 1991.131

*Cloistered Indian Pipes
Botanical,* 1989
Lamp-worked and encased
glass; 15.5 x 7.1 (6¹⁄₁₆ x 2¾)
Mike and Annie Belkin
Collection

Cactus Botanical, 1990
Lamp-worked and encased
glass; 15.2 x 7.6 x 7.6 (6 x
3 x 3)
Mike and Annie Belkin
Collection

Paphiopedium with Spirit,
1991
Lamp-worked and encased
glass; h. 5.3 (2¹⁄₁₆), diam. 8
(3⅛)
Virginia Q. Foley
Collection

■ 53

Mountain Laurel Botanical,
1994
Lamp-worked and encased
glass; 12.7 x 8 x 7 (5 x 3⅛
x 2¾)
Mike and Annie Belkin
Collection

*Coronet Botanical with
Insects,* 1995
Lamp-worked and encased
glass; 11.9 x 7.2 (4¹¹⁄₁₆ x
2¹³⁄₁₆)
Mike and Annie Belkin
Collection

Environmental with Turtle,
1995 (turtle by Rick
Ayotte)
Lamp-worked and encased
glass; 5.6 x 8.4 (2³⁄₁₆ x 3¼)
Mike and Annie Belkin
Collection

Jack Ink

Landscape 1075, 1983
Cast glass; 19.7 x 15.6 x
3.9 (7¾ x 6⅛ x 1½)
The Cleveland Museum of
Art, The Harold T. Clark
Educational Extension
Fund 1984.1128

Ink (1944–) was born in Canton, and members of his family continue to live in northeastern Ohio. He studied at Kent State University and with Harvey Littleton at the University of Wisconsin in the early 1970s, but at the end of that decade he was an artist-in-residence at the firm of J. & L. Lobmeyr in Vienna, and since then has lived in central Europe. His specialty is richly colored glass, often iridescent, with occasional suggestions of landscape designs, generally incorporated into vessel forms. His work seems inspired by that of Tiffany and other turn-of-the-century glass artists.

Untitled, 1987
Mold-blown glass with
metal frame; 10.6 x 21.1
(4⅛ x 8⁵⁄₁₆)
Heinz and Elizabeth Wolf
Collection

Mark Vance

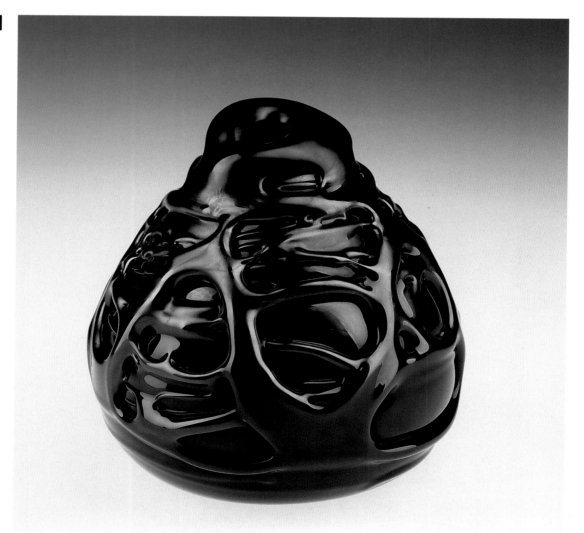

Vase, 1977
Blown glass; h. 16.5 (6½),
diam. 16.5 (6½)
The Cleveland Museum of
Art, Gift of George and
Lois Vance 1996.263

Cleveland native Vance (1947–) was a student at Bowling Green State University during the late 1960s and
early 1970s. At that time he studied glassblowing with Dominick Labino. From 1974 to 1978 he operated Vance
Glassworks in Peninsula, Ohio.

Brent Kee Young

Untitled, 1977
Blown glass; 23.7 x 13.9
(9⁵/₁₆ x 5⁷/₁₆)
Heinz and Elizabeth Wolf
Collection

Born in Los Angeles, Young (1946–) studied at Alfred (New York) and San Jose State (California) universities. For many years he has headed the glass department of the Cleveland Institute of Art. He is perhaps best known for glass of simple cylindrical forms with inclusions that suggest fossilized animals.

Fossil Fantasy: Fishin' with Bill, 1978
Blown glass; h. 13.7 (5⅜),
diam. 11.4 (4½)
The Cleveland Museum of
Art, The Harold T. Clark
Educational Extension
Fund 1978.1025

Vase, 1982
Mold-blown glass; 20.3 x
21 x 19 (8 x 8¼ x 7½)
The Cleveland Museum of
Art, Louis D. Kacalieff,
M.D., Fund 1982.60

Mary Shaffer

Inverted Cube, 1991
Bronze and slumped glass;
part 1: 98.5 x 31.1 (38¾ x
12¼); part 2: 97.2 x 34.4
(38¼ x 13½)
Helen and David
Kangesser Collection

Like a number of artists concerned with glass as a medium of expression, Shaffer (1947–) studied at the Rhode
Island School of Design. Her work customarily involves slumped glass and metal in the creation of large-scale
sculptures.

Figure Standing on Dice,
1989
Mold-blown, cut, ground,
and polished glass; 72.4 x
21.5 (28½ x 8⁷⁄₁₆)
Jules and Fran Belkin
Collection

Palusky (1942–) mastered a number of glassmaking techniques, as have many glass artists trained in the 1960s. His
mature work consists of sculptures often employing glass
made in several ways and sometimes combined with
other materials, particularly stone.

John Lewis

Zig Zag Micro Pedestal,
1991
Cast glass; 85.1 x 24.2
(33½ x 9½)
Ann and Robert Friedman
Collection

Lewis (1942–) received his training in glassmaking at the
University of California, Berkeley, in the department
founded by Marvin Lipofsky. Lewis's early work focused
on blown glass vessel forms, but more recently he has
created large-scale abstract sculptures of cast glass.

Dan Dailey

Les Danseurs, 1979
Pâte-de-verre; 36 x 35.8
(14⅛ x 14¹⁄₁₆)
Francine and Benson
Pilloff Collection

Jazz Man, 1988
Blown glass with enamel
decoration; 39.2 x 27
(15⁷⁄₁₆ x 10⅝)
Francine and Benson
Pilloff Collection

Buzz, 1990
Blown glass; 28.8 x 54
(11⅝⁄₁₆ x 21¼)
Clarine and Harvey Saks
Collection

A native of Philadelphia, Dailey (1947–) received his first professional training at the College of Art in that city, but next, and probably more significant for his role as a glassmaker, he studied at the Rhode Island School of Design in the early 1970s, at a time when it was an important center of the nascent studio glass movement. Although he has frequently taught special courses, Dailey has essentially been an independent glass artist living in New England. His work is characterized by great technical variety, but almost always his productions include an element of humor.

Richard Marquis

Teapot Trophy, 1989
Blown glass; 80.3 x 26.7
(31⅝ x 10½)
Mike and Annie Belkin
Collection

Marquis (1945–) received his education at the University of California, Berkeley, in the late 1960s, and from 1977 to 1983 he taught at U.C.L.A. Since then he has continued to make southern California the locus of his glass-making activities. Marquis often creates sculptures that appear to be at least in part functional vessels but, in fact, are not. He incorporates found material in his compositions, but he also makes use of slices of glass canes of his own manufacture to create objects in the tradition of Venetian *mille fleur* glass.

Thomas Patti

Compacted Blue with Green, 1986, 1986
Fused, hand-shaped, ground, and polished glass; 9.5 x 13.6 (3¾ x 5⁵⁄₁₆)
Private collection, Cleveland

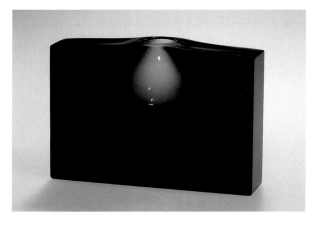  

A Massachusetts native, Patti (1943–) received his training at the Pratt Institute in New York City. He specializes in small but monumental sculptures made by fusing glass.

Michael Pavlik

Kunsterstruction, 1993
Cut and polished glass;
81.3 x 45.8 x 45.8 (32 x
18 x 18)
Dan and Linda Rocker
Silverberg Collection

Born in Prague, Pavlik (1941–) received his earliest training there. After coming to the United States, he worked
at the Penland School of Crafts. He produces abstract

glass sculptures unusually composed of linked elements of
simple geometric forms with highly polished surfaces. At
least some color is included in most of his pieces.

Whirling Red Triangles,
1994
Cut and polished glass;
38.1 x 40.7 x 30.6 (15 x
16 x 12)
Dan and Linda Rocker
Silverberg Collection

Sydney Cash

Harmonic Disposition of the Souls Held Dear, Brings Ionic Interspersion in a Man's Right Ear, 1984
Slumped glass and brass;
35.2 x 46.4 (13¹³⁄₁₆ x 18¼)
Mike and Annie Belkin Collection

Royal Emotion, 1988
Slumped glass; 33.9 x 28 (13⁵⁄₁₆ x 11)
Dan and Linda Rocker Silverberg Collection

A native of Detroit, Cash (1941–) is a graduate of Wayne State University in that city. He is best known for his carefully controlled slumped glass in which a wire armature has been used to regulate the pattern of the glass as it is partially melted and sags. Most recently he has also produced small sculptures employing found objects in mirrored boxes, creating spatial illusions.

José Chardiet

Mesa Series, 1987
Sand-cast glass and enamel;
81.8 x 21 (32³⁄₁₆ x 8¼)
Mike and Annie Belkin
Collection

Born in Havana, Chardiet (1956–) was trained in the United States, receiving an M.F.A. from Kent State University in 1983. He employs a wide variety of techniques in the production and decoration of vessels and sculptures, but casting seems his usual mode of achieving basic forms, and sandblasting is often at least a part of his decorative vocabulary.

Untitled, 1992
Blown glass and enamel;
44.1 x 31.2 (17⅜ x 12¼)
Mike and Annie Belkin
Collection

Sally Rogers

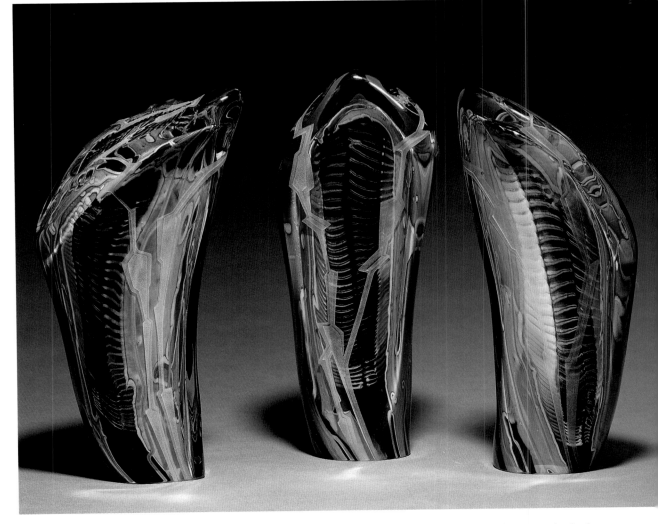

Moraine, 1992
Mold-blown glass; part 1:
37.7 x 18.5 (14¹³⁄₁₆ x 7¼),
part 2: 39.3 x 18.2 (15⁷⁄₁₆
x 7⅛), part 3: 38 x 19.6
(14¹⁵⁄₁₆ x 7¹¹⁄₁₆)
Private collection

Rogers (1960–) received an M.F.A. from Kent State University in 1989 and subsequently has been associated with the Penland School of Crafts. She has tried her hand at several glassmaking techniques, but recently she has been working with cast pâte-de-verre combined with steel elements.

Judith Schaechter

Death in the Flesh, 1989
Stained glass; 44.1 x 76.9
(17⅜ x 30¼)
Francine and Benson
Pilloff Collection

Schaechter (1961–) was in her second year at the Rhode Island School of Design when she first tried her hand at making stained glass under the tutelage of Ursula Huth. It proved to be a medium that suited her aesthetic and expressive aims perfectly and has continued to dominate her artistic production. The subject matter of Schaechter's stained-glass compositions tends to be painful and psychologically intense.

William R. McKinney

Bill's Ball, 1986
Blown glass; 12.2 x 12.2 x
9 (4¾ x 4¾ x 3½)
The Cleveland Museum of
Art, The Harold T. Clark
Educational Extension
Fund 1987.1009

McKinney (1958–) was born in Ravenna, Ohio, and received his education as a glassmaker largely at Bowling Green State University. He has worked with a variety of glass techniques and has expressed an interest in the optical qualities of thick glass.

20th-Century Primitive,
1987
Cast glass; 26.1 x 10.8 x 12
(10¼ x 4¼ x 4¹¹⁄₁₆)
The Cleveland Museum of
Art, The Harold T. Clark
Educational Extension
Fund 1987.1008

Mark Sudduth

Inside-Out II, 1986
Cast glass; 27.3 x 14.7 x
9.6 (10¾ x 5¾ x 3¾)
The Cleveland Museum of
Art, The Sarah Stern
Michael Fund 1987.68

A native of Dover, Ohio, Sudduth (1960–) has focused his glassmaking activities on Cleveland, first as a student of Brent Kee Young at the Cleveland Institute of Art and, more recently, as an independent artist and sometime teacher. He is well equipped technically and produces both blown and cast glass.

Daniel Clayman

Untitled, 1990
Cast glass and patinated
copper; 55.9 x 36.3 (22
x 14¼)
Mike and Annie Belkin
Collection

Clayman (1957–) received a degree from the Rhode
Island School of Design in 1986. He produces symmetri-
cal cast glass sculptures that suggest vessel shapes. The colors are muted, the surfaces matte, and metal is often
used to vary surface color and texture.

John Brekke

*No Me Puede Quitar Lo
Bailado,* 1996
Blown glass with sand-
blasted decoration; 30.7
x 25.1 (12¹/₁₆ x 9⅞)
Dan and Linda Rocker
Silverberg Collection

Brekke (1955–) attended Illinois State University and
graduated from the University of Wisconsin, Madison, in
1978. He makes vessels in which words perform both a visual and a cognitive function to reflect contemporary
life. His pieces are blown and then engraved and acid
etched.

Joyce Scott

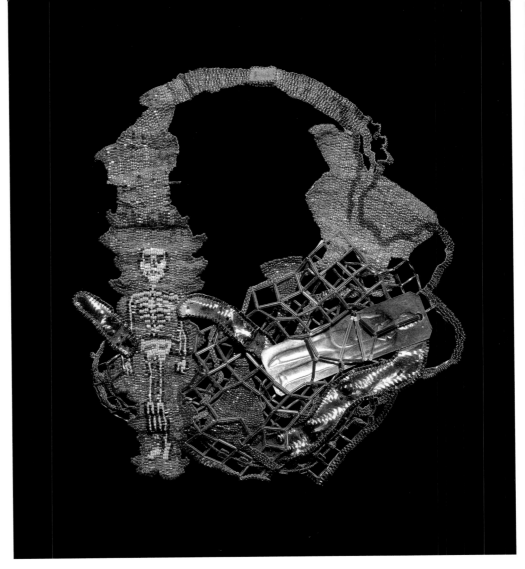

Flaming Skeleton Series #1,
1993
Mixed media and glass
beads; 33.6 x 28.4 (13³⁄₁₆
x 11³⁄₁₆)
Francine and Benson
Pilloff Collection

With a B.F.A. from the Maryland Institute College of Art in her native Baltimore, Scott (1948–) earned an M.F.A. from the Instituto Allende in San Miguel Allende, Mexico. In addition to jewelry made of glass beads, she also has created fiber art and mixed-media objects, often with specific subject matter of a contentious nature.

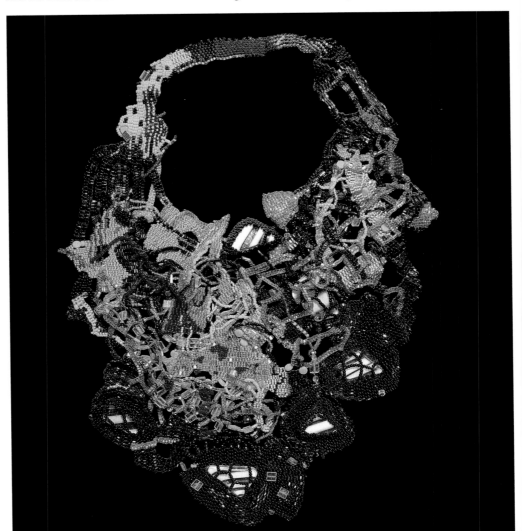

Night and Crystal, 1993
Mixed media and glass
beads; 36.7 x 26.7 (14⁷⁄₁₆
x 10½)
Francine and Benson
Pilloff Collection

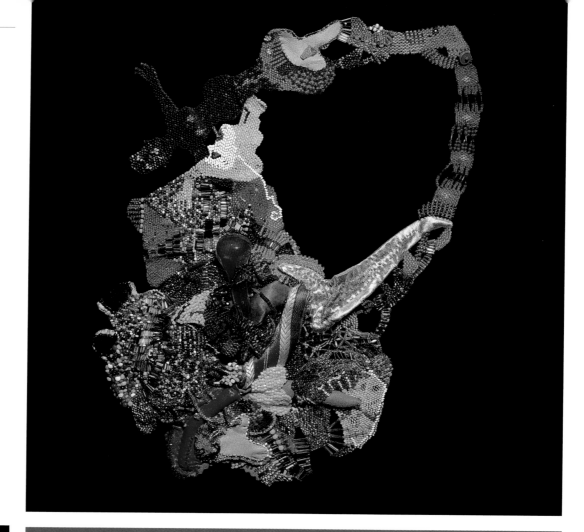

Holocaust, 1994
Mixed media and glass
beads; 39.7 x 30.5 (15⅝
x 12)
Francine and Benson
Pilloff Collection

Kari Russell-Pool
and Marc Petrovic

Flush, 1995
Lamp-worked and blown
glass; 49.2 x 35.6 x 20.3
(19⅜ x 14 x 8)
Lorrie and Alvin Magid
Collection

Although glassmakers Russell-Pool (1967–) and Petrovic (1967–) sometimes work independently, their efforts are more often cooperative. Russell-Pool constructs cages or arborlike structures with lamp work—melted and blown glass manipulated in small quantities using a limited source of heat. Petrovic supplies blown glass elements, often birds. On an expressive level the results are unique to these artists.

Dante Marioni

Giant Whopper Vase, 1992
Blown glass; 111.8 x 36.2
(44 x 14¼)
Francine and Benson
Pilloff Collection

Red Leaf, about 1995
Blown glass; 85.8 x 18.8
(33¾ x 7⅜)
Private collection

Ivory and Black, 1996
Blown glass; part 1: 67.3 x
22 x 15.9 (26½ x 8⅝ x
6¼), part 2: 76.8 x 17.2 x
15.9 (30¼ x 6¾ x 6¼), part
3: 37.5 x 38.5 x 27.3 (14¾

x 15⅛ x 10¾)
Mike and Annie Belkin
Collection

The son of a glass artist, Marioni (1964–) began blowing
glass at an early age. His repertoire of forms is limited and
decoration is confined to bands of glass of contrasting
color. Within these limitations, however, he strives for
perfectly formed glass vessels, sometimes of monumental
proportions.

Structure #8, 1983
Cast glass with copper
overlay; 94.7 x 38.4
(37¼ x 15⅛)
Francine and Benson
Pilloff Collection

Although born in Brooklyn, New York, Ben Tré (1949–) has long been associated with Providence, first as a student at the Rhode Island School of Design and later as the locale of his studio. He is a sculptor who chooses glass as his medium, and casting is his technique for achieving basic forms. He creates detail and texture with sandblasting, cutting, and polishing, sometimes also adding metal and gilding.

Fifth Figure, 1987
Cast glass, copper, and
gold leaf; 213.4 x 76.2 x
18.6 (84 x 30 x 7⁵⁄₁₆)
The Cleveland Museum of
Art, Gift of Mike and
Annie Belkin 1993.197

Wrapped Form #2, 1993
Cast glass and iron
powder; 142.2 x 62.3
(56 x 24½)
Francine and Benson
Pilloff Collection

Michael Aschenbrenner

Untitled, 1991
Hot manipulated glass and
mixed media; 49.2 x 70.7
(19⅜ x 27¹³⁄₁₆)
Francine and Benson
Pilloff Collection

Aschenbrenner (1949–) was born in California and, after
service in Vietnam, attended universities in California
and Minneapolis. He is best known for sculptures that
include representations in glass of damaged bones, subject
matter said to have been inspired by his time in the army.

Steven Weinberg

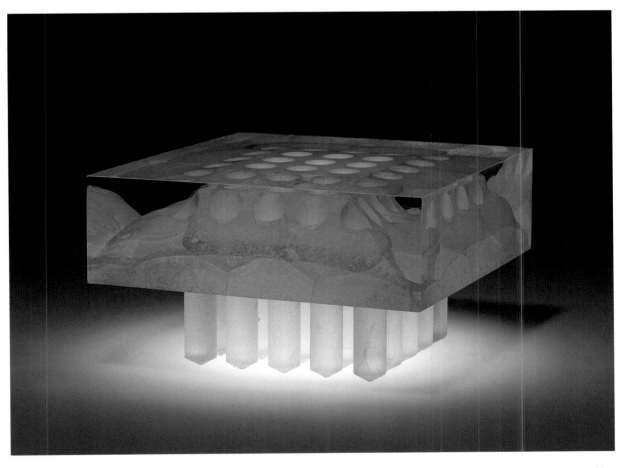

Untitled, 1984
Cast glass, polished; 12.9
x 21.7 (5¹⁄₁₆ x 8½)
Mike and Annie Belkin
Collection

Initially Weinberg (1954–) trained as a ceramist at Alfred
University. He then went to the Rhode Island School of
Design where he took up glassmaking. He is a sculptor in
glass who produces his basic forms through casting and
then alters and enriches them with a variety of techniques
including sandblasting, grinding, and cutting. Many of his
works are inspired by architecture. Cubic in shape, they
include elements that suggest columns, parapets, stair-
cases, and other architectural elements.

Untitled, 1988
Cast glass, polished; 20.9
x 20.9 (8³⁄₁₆ x 8³⁄₁₆)
Clarine and Harvey Saks
Collection

Untitled, 1991
Cast glass, polished; 23.5
x 22.5 x 22.5 (9¼ x 8¹³⁄₁₆
x 8¹³⁄₁₆)
The Cleveland Museum of
Art, Seventy-fifth anniver-
sary gift of Annie and
Mike Belkin 1992.101

Daniel Rothenfeld

Chrysalis, 1983
Laminated plate glass; 58.3
x 19.8 (22¹⁵⁄₁₆ x 7¾)
Dan and Linda Rocker
Silverberg Collection

Rothenfeld (1953–) studied first at the Rhode Island
School of Design, receiving a B.F.A. in 1977. Later he
earned a master's degree at Kent State University. He has
devised a personal mode of creating glass sculpture in
which roughly shaped horizontal sheets of glass are
stacked vertically to suggest forms, usually the human
figure.

William Carlson

Prägnanz Series, 1987
Granite and cast, lami-
nated, and polished glass;
52.1 x 50.8 x 12.7 (20½ x
20 x 5)
Mike and Annie Belkin
Collection

Contrapuntal Series, 1989
Granite and cast, lami-
nated, and polished glass;
52.1 x 38.1 x 38.1 (20½ x
15 x 15)
The Cleveland Museum of
Art, Gift of Mike and
Annie Belkin 1991.212

Contrapuntal Series, 1992
Granite and cast, laminated, and polished glass;
53.3 x 47 (21 x 18½)
Mike and Annie Belkin
Collection

An Ohio native, Carlson (1950–) studied at the Art Students' League in New York City, the Cleveland Institute of Art, and Alfred University. He has wide experience with various glassmaking techniques, but the work for which he is best known combines laminated polished glass set into regularly shaped granite units joined to form rectilinear abstract sculptures.

Paul Seide

Radio Lights, 1986
Radioactivated neon; part
1: 52.7 x 26 (20¾ x 10³⁄₁₆),
part 2: 32.1 x 21 (12⅝ x
8¼)
Mike and Annie Belkin
Collection

Seide (1949–), a New Yorker by birth, was trained at the
Egani Neon Glassblowing School in that city and then
studied at the University of Wisconsin, Madison, where
he received a degree in fine arts in 1974. His sculptures,
which are varied in form, often employ activated gases,
the basic principle of neon lighting.

Christopher Ries

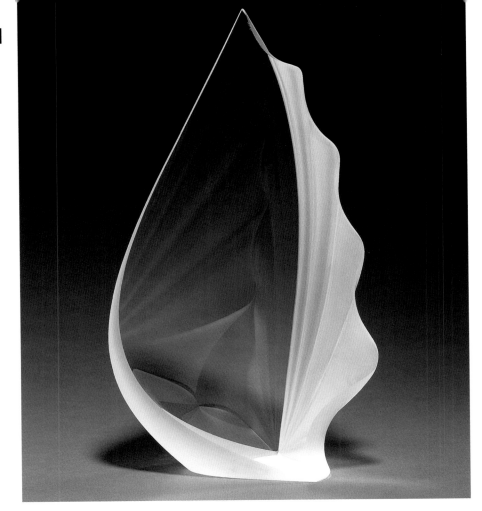

Satin Pleats
Cut and polished glass;
44.5 x 24.8 (17½ x 9¾)
Private collection

In the 1970s Ries (1952–) studied with Littleton at the University of Wisconsin, focusing on glassblowing. More recently, he has usually employed colorless optical glass he cuts and polishes to create sculptures that, viewed in their entirety, are generally simple abstract shapes. When seen at close range and from various angles, the refraction or reflection of light within the body of the work creates internal designs.

Jon Kuhn

143 Linda, 1993
Laminated, cut, and polished glass; 25.4 x 25.4 x 25.4 (10 x 10 x 10)
Dan and Linda Rocker Silverberg Collection

In his early work Kuhn (1949–) created glass suggesting the rough surfaces of uncut and unpolished stone. More recently, he has worked with optical glass built up by lamination from a small-scale core to a larger rectilinear form. These pieces rely for their effect on the brilliance of clear glass, though in some cases color has been added to the core construction.

Clear Skies, 1993
Laminated, cut, and polished
glass; 76.2 x 76.2 (30 x 30)
Ester Goldsmith Collection

Kreg Kallenberger

Cuneiform Series, 1986
Blown, cut, and polished
glass; 17.4 x 18.6 (6¹³⁄₁₆ x
7⁵⁄₁₆)
Mike and Annie Belkin
Collection

Kallenberger (1950–) has centered his professional life at
the University of Tulsa. He creates abstract glass sculptures using a wide variety of techniques with results that
are at times rough-hewn, at others precisely finished and
polished.

Michael M. Glancy

Convoluted Continuum,
1986
Blown and sandblasted
glass with copper electroplate; 14.1 x 12.2 (5½ x
4¾)
Mike and Annie Belkin
Collection

A native of Detroit, Glancy (1950–) attended schools in
Denver and the Rhode Island School of Design. He is
best known for glass with designs in deep relief combined
with metal coatings covering part of the surface, the
whole executed using irregular forms that suggest organic
sources of inspiration.

David R. Huchthausen

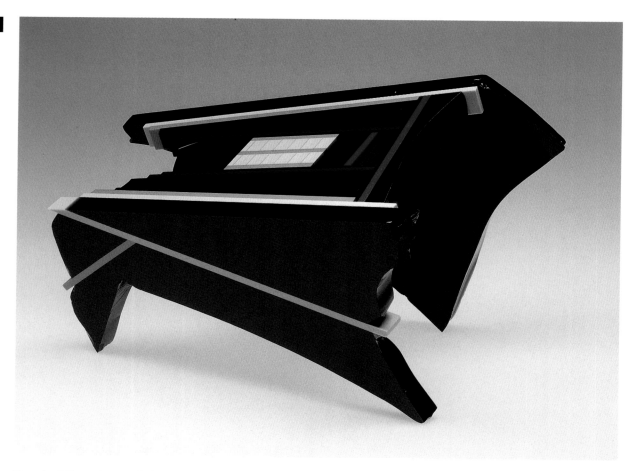

Leitungs Scherbe, 1986
Laminated, cut, and polished glass; 32.4 x 50.2
(12¾ x 19¾)
Jules and Fran Belkin
Collection

Born in Wisconsin, Huchthausen (1951–) received his early training there, including a stint at the University of Wisconsin in the department headed by Littleton. Later he studied and then taught at Illinois State University with Joel Philip Myers. Huchthausen's earliest work was blown glass, but more recently he has made sculptures of laminated glass.

Sonja Blomdahl

Blue/Ruby/Violet, 1991
Blown glass; 31.5 x 28.3
(12⅜ x 11⅛)
Lorrie and Alvin Magid
Collection

Blomdahl (1952–), who has worked in the Seattle area, makes symmetrical vessel forms with bands of variously colored glass as their only decoration. She says of her work, "I just want to make the most beautiful object I can." In almost every respect, her glass stands apart from that of her American contemporaries.

Ocean Travel, 1993
Painted glass and mixed
media; 139.6 x 106.7 x
81.3 (55 x 42 x 32)
Dan and Linda Rocker
Silverberg Collection

Statom (1953–) makes use of glass, but its physical prop-
erties do not dominate his work. He is a sculptor, insofar
as he creates three-dimensional forms resembling such
structures as chairs and ladders. His surfaces are frequently
freely painted, and the found objects he uses make many
of his pieces three-dimensional collages. Although difficult to classify, Statom's work seems to have an authentic
originality.

Judy Jensen

On the Road, 1993
Reverse painting on glass;
85.7 x 81.6 (33¾ x 32⅛)
Francine and Benson
Pilloff Collection

A Texan by birth, Jensen (1953–) attended the University of Texas. She is essentially a painter who uses glass as her canvas, creating low reliefs of varied shape and with a smooth, hard surface of glass providing an appropriate support for highly imaginative, dreamlike subjects executed in vivid enamel colors.

Richard Bernstein

Dance Studio, 1984
Laminated glass with
enamel painting; 40.7 x
44.5 (16 x 17½)
Mike and Annie Belkin
Collection

Born in Newark, New Jersey, Bernstein (1952–) received a degree from the Philadelphia College of Art in 1968. He has produced a wide variety of glass including laminated low reliefs. Painterly surface decoration almost always characterizes his work, and he frequently introduces a note of humor into his designs.

Jay Musler

Ugly Bowl, 1989
Slumped glass, plate-glass
mosaic, and applied oil
pigments; h. 41.3 (16¼),
diam. 54.6 (21½)
Mike and Annie Belkin
Collection

Musler (1949–), a native of northern California, studied with Marvin Lipofsky at the California College of Arts and Crafts. In his glassmaking Musler has focused attention on surface decoration to create pieces with a particular emotional resonance. He often uses commercial glass blanks that he modifies by cutting and slumping and then decorates with oil paint and sandblasting.

Doug Anderson

Hide and Seek, 1988
Pâte-de-verre; 25.4 x 31.2
(10 x 12¼)
Mike and Annie Belkin
Collection

Dragonflies, 1991
Pâte-de-verre; 34.3 x 35.6
x 7.6 (13½ x 14 x 3)
Mike and Annie Belkin
Collection

Anderson (1952–) is one of a small group of American glass artists who have taken up the technique of pâte-de-verre, ground glass mixed with pigments and heated in a mold until they fuse. This method of fabrication was revived in France in the late nineteenth century, and Anderson has made use of both the process and, to a degree, the style of the French work. He sometimes employs living things in creating molds in which to cast elements of his pieces.

Karla Trinkley

Untitled, 1986
Pâte-de-verre; h. 29.9
(11¾), diam. 31.8 (12½)
Mike and Annie Belkin
Collection

Pinky, 1994
Pâte-de-verre; h. 30
(11¹³⁄₁₆), diam. 51.9 (20⁷⁄₁₆)
Mike and Annie Belkin
Collection

In her work Trinkley (1956–) combines several traditions to produce pieces of originality and distinction. First there is the material, pâte-de-verre, which was used by the first French studio glassmaker, Henri Cros. Ground glass and pigments are mixed together and then fired in a mold. Second, like certain late works of Frederick Carder, her cast glass is based in form on an ancient Roman carved cage vessel, a *diatretum*. The results are both attractive and technically accomplished.

Pregnant Bust Jones, about
1995
Blown glass; 84.9 x 47
(33⁷⁄₁₆ x 18½)
Private collection

Powell (1951–) trained as a ceramist, a path many
glassmakers have followed. Only within the last decade
has glass become his medium of choice. As a glass artist
Powell has devoted himself to free blown decorative
vessels, often of large scale.

Toots Zynsky

Angry Birds from the Birds of Paradise Series, 1987
Pulled and fused glass threads; 13.7 x 29.5 (5⅜ x 11⁹⁄₁₆)
Mike and Annie Belkin Collection

Italian Chaos IV
Pulled and fused glass threads; 19.4 x 38.1 (7⅝ x 15)
Private collection

Zynsky (1951–) was born in Boston and educated at the Rhode Island School of Design. Although trained in a wide variety of glassmaking techniques, the works for which she is best known are bowl-shaped vessels made of fused glass threads. Recently much of her time has been spent abroad.

Paris Chaos, 1994
Pulled and fused glass
threads; 15.6 x 38.2 (6⅛
x 15)
Ann and Robert Friedman
Collection

Ginny Ruffner

*Tunnel of Love Wears
Heartbreak Pajamas,* 1989
Lamp-worked glass and
paint; 30.3 x 63.2 (11¹⁵⁄₁₆
x 24⅞)
Francine and Benson
Pilloff Collection

Jewels of Spring, 1991
Lamp-worked glass and
paint; 44.7 x 42.6 (17⅟₁₆
x 16¾)
Helen and David
Kangesser Collection

A native of Georgia, Ruffner (1952–) studied painting at
the University of Georgia. Not surprisingly, even though
she now makes lamp-work glass compositions of complex
form, painting remains important in that her glass pieces
customarily have painted surfaces, often with detailed,
realistic scenes. The imagination with which she endows
the subject matter of her pieces has made Ruffner's reputation as a glass artist.

Cloaked Doll, 1983
Blown glass and wood;
34.4 x 9.4 (13½ x 3¹¹⁄₁₆)
Francine and Benson
Pilloff Collection

Untitled (Bowl with Birds),
1983
Blown glass and wire
drawings; 16.6 x 19.8 (6½
x 7¾)
Francine and Benson
Pilloff Collection

Pear, 1992
Blown glass; 58.5 x 38.8
(23 x 15¼)
Francine and Benson
Pilloff Collection

Mace (1949–) and Kirkpatrick (1952–) enjoy a long-
standing partnership that has resulted in the production of
diverse pieces, some of them sculptures that combine
wood and glass, others made entirely of glass. While
their work is technically varied, its expressive intensity of
emotion makes it unique. Mace and Kirkpatrick live in the
Seattle area and have on occasion participated in Dale
Chihuly's glass productions.

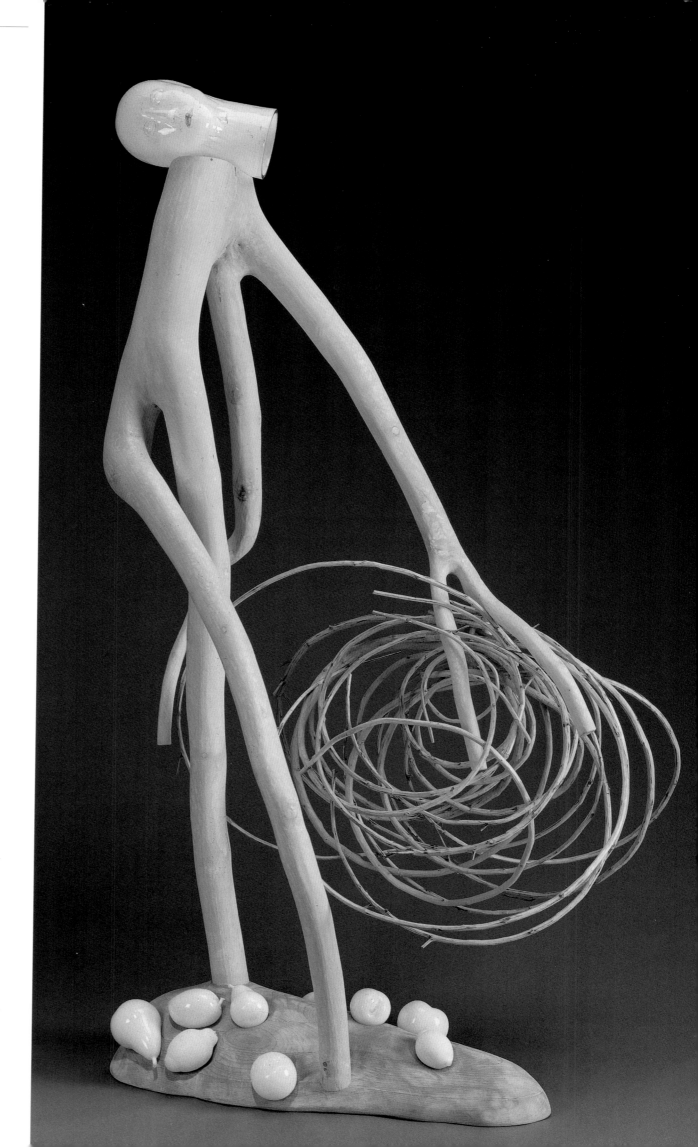

Seasonal Sphire, 1994
Blown glass and wood;
208.2 x 116.8 x 58.4 (82
x 46 x 23)
Francine and Benson
Pilloff Collection

Vas Hermeticum, 1990
Blown glass with enamel
and metal-leaf decoration;
73.5 x 24 (28¹⁵⁄₁₆ x 9⁷⁄₁₆)
Francine and Benson
Pilloff Collection

Carlson (1952–), born in New York, has for most of his
career been associated with the Pilchuck Glass School
near Seattle where he studied with Flora C. Mace and
Joey Kirkpatrick and Dan Dailey. Carlson works with
blown or cast glass forms, many of which suggest figures
or architecture. These shapes are then richly embellished
with colored enamel decoration, often including symbols
suggesting an esoteric mysticism.

Mary Kay Simoni

No Mo, 1989
Laminated glass with plas-
tic additions; 52.9 x 25.6
(20¹³⁄₁₆ x 10¹⁄₁₆)
Heinz and Elizabeth Wolf
Collection

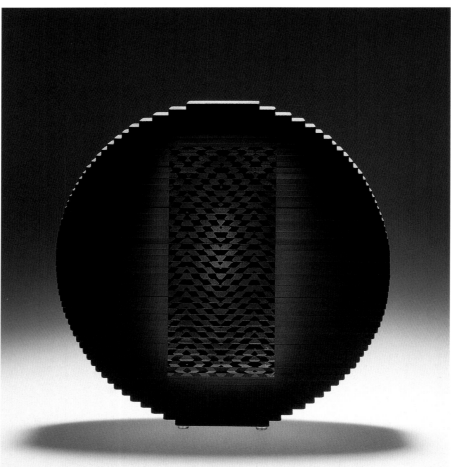

(W)Hole TV Window, 1996
Laminated glass; 32 x 31.7
(12⁹⁄₁₆ x 12⁷⁄₁₆)
Dan and Linda Rocker
Silverberg Collection

Simoni (1955–) attended the Cleveland Institute of Art
and Kent State University and lives in the Cleveland area.

Her pieces are made of laminated glass, with their surfaces
sandblasted. She operates her own glassmaking facility.

Hank Adams

Head with Gears, 1986
Cast glass and oxidized
metal; 50.8 x 31.8 x 31.8
(20 x 12½ x 12½)
Mike and Annie Belkin
Collection

Adams (1956–) works largely with cast glass to create images that lean toward the grotesque. His work has been widely exhibited and well received both in this country and abroad, especially in Japan.

Janusz Walentynowicz

The Bundle, 1994 or 1995
Cast glass and paint; 50 x
39.8 (19¹¹⁄₁₆ x 15⅝)
Ann and Robert Friedman
Collection

Born in Poland, Walentynowicz (1956–) studied first in Denmark and later at Illinois State University with Joel Philip Myers. Walentynowicz creates sculptures chiefly of glass but sometimes with other materials as well. The human figure or parts thereof are usually included in his compositions.

The Cultivation, 1993
Cast glass and metal; 132
x 17.8 (52 x 7)
Dan and Linda Rocker
Silverberg Collection

Like so many glass artists, Grebe (1957–) first focused on ceramics, receiving a diploma in that field from the Massachusetts College of Art, Boston, in 1980. Later at the Tyler School of Art near Philadelphia, she added glass to her repertoire of media. Grebe is primarily a sculptor in glass, and most of her works in this material have at least the suggestion of figural representation.

Sherry Markovitz

Swoosh, 1991
Mixed media with beads,
papier-mâché, and fiber-
glass; 238.6 x 12.7 x 22.9
(94 x 5 x 9)
Francine and Benson
Pilloff Collection

Markovitz (1947–) creates beaded sculptures, sometimes
developing clearly recognizable images such as animals
and, at other times, abstract shapes. She strings the beads
and then sews or glues them to the desired form.

Steve Tobin

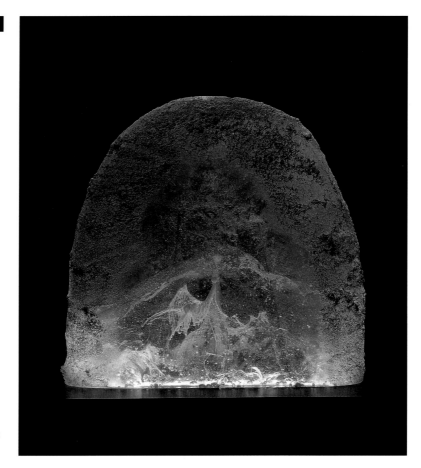

Doorway, 1992
Sand-cast glass with
injected hot inclusions,
polished; 41.5 x 43
(16⁵⁄₁₆ x 16¹⁵⁄₁₆)
Ann and Robert Friedman
Collection

Tobin (1957–) graduated from Tulane University, New Orleans, in 1979 with a major in mathematics, but by that year he was already an accomplished glass artist. He has produced significant pieces employing both cast and blown glass. Recently, he has executed some large constructions that include glass but go well beyond the usual definition of glass sculpture since other materials are involved and the results are only partially beholden to the specific characteristics of glass.

William Morris

Petroglyph Vessel, 1989
Blown glass; 55.5 x 50.1
(21¹³⁄₁₆ x 19¹¹⁄₁₆)
Clarine and Harvey Saks
Collection

Standing Stone, 1989
Mold-blown glass; 118.1
x 28 (46½ x 11)
Francine and Benson
Pilloff Collection

Morris (1957–) received his training as one of Dale Chihuly's team of assistants. In the 1980s Morris began producing independently and has created several series of glass sculptures: the early "Stones" and, later, the Egyptian-inspired canopic jars and objects suggesting archaeological and ethnographic artifacts. Technically accomplished, he frequently combines cast and blown glass in pieces with complex surface ornament.

Burial Urn with Tool, 1991
Blown and cast glass; 51.4
x 57.8 (20¼ x 22¾)
Francine and Benson
Pilloff Collection

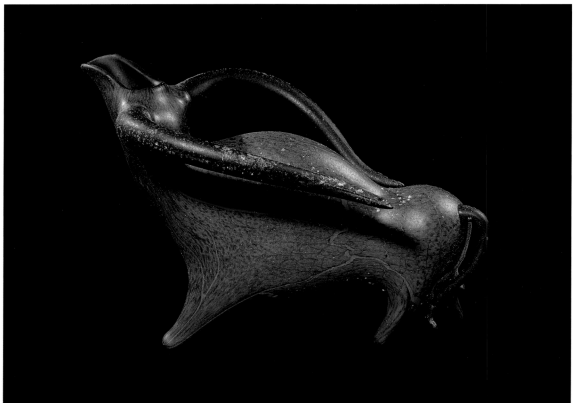

Rhyton Bull, 1996
Blown and manipulated
glass; 17.8 x 26 (7 x 10³⁄₁₆)
Ann and Robert Friedman
Collection

Canopic Jar—Mountain Lion, about 1995
Blown and cast glass; 63.2 x 22.3 (24⅞ x 8¾)
Private collection

Checklist

Hank Adams (American, b. 1956)
Head with Gears, 1986
Cast glass and oxidized metal; 50.8 x 31.8 x 31.8
(20 x 12½ x 12½)
Mike and Annie Belkin Collection

Doug Anderson (American, b. 1952)
Dragonflies, 1991
Pâte-de-verre; 34.3 x 35.6 x 7.6 (13½ x 14 x 3)
Mike and Annie Belkin Collection

Doug Anderson (American, b. 1952)
Hide and Seek, 1988
Pâte-de-verre; 25.4 x 31.2 (10 x 12¼)
Mike and Annie Belkin Collection

Michael Aschenbrenner (American, b. 1949)
Untitled, 1991
Hot manipulated glass and mixed media; 49.2 x 70.7
(19⅜ x 27¹³⁄₁₆)
Francine and Benson Pilloff Collection

Howard Ben Tré (American, b. 1949)
Fifth Figure, 1987
Cast glass, copper, and gold leaf; 213.4 x 76.2 x 18.6
(84 x 30 x 7⁵⁄₁₆)
The Cleveland Museum of Art, Gift of Mike and
Annie Belkin 1993.197

Howard Ben Tré (American, b. 1949)
Structure #8, 1983
Cast glass with copper overlay; 94.7 x 38.4 (37¼
x 15⅛)
Francine and Benson Pilloff Collection

Howard Ben Tré (American, b. 1949)
Wrapped Form #2, 1993
Cast glass and iron powder; 142.2 x 62.3 (56 x 24½)
Francine and Benson Pilloff Collection

Richard Bernstein (American, b. 1952)
Dance Studio, 1984
Laminated glass with enamel painting; 40.7 x 44.5
(16 x 17½)
Mike and Annie Belkin Collection

Sonja Blomdahl (American, b. 1952)
Blue/Ruby/Violet, 1991
Blown glass; 31.5 x 28.3 (12⅜ x 11⅛)
Lorrie and Alvin Magid Collection

John Brekke (American, b. 1955)
No Me Puede Quitar Lo Bailado, 1996
Blown glass with sandblasted decoration; 30.7 x 25.1
(12¹⁄₁₆ x 9⅞)
Dan and Linda Rocker Silverberg Collection

Robert Carlson (American, b. 1952)
Vas Hermeticum, 1990
Blown glass with enamel and metal-leaf decoration;
73.5 x 24 (28¹⁵⁄₁₆ x 9⁷⁄₁₆)
Francine and Benson Pilloff Collection

William Carlson (American, b. 1950)
Contrapuntal Series, 1989
Granite and cast, laminated, and polished glass; 52.1
x 38.1 x 38.1 (20½ x 15 x 15)
The Cleveland Museum of Art, Gift of Mike and
Annie Belkin 1991.212

William Carlson (American, b. 1950)
Contrapuntal Series, 1992
Granite and cast, laminated, and polished glass;
53.3 x 47 (21 x 18½)
Mike and Annie Belkin Collection

William Carlson (American, b. 1950)
Prägnanz Series, 1987
Granite and cast, laminated, and polished glass;
52.1 x 50.8 x 12.7 (20½ x 20 x 5)
Mike and Annie Belkin Collection

Sydney Cash (American, b. 1941)
*Harmonic Disposition of the Souls Held Dear, Brings Ionic
Interspersion in a Man's Right Ear*, 1984
Slumped glass and brass; 35.2 x 46.4 (13¹³⁄₁₆ x 18¼)
Mike and Annie Belkin Collection

Sydney Cash (American, b. 1941)
Royal Emotion, 1988
Slumped glass; 33.9 x 28 (13⁵⁄₁₆ x 11)
Dan and Linda Rocker Silverberg Collection

José Chardiet (American, b. Cuba, 1956)
Mesa Series, 1987
Sand-cast glass and enamel; 81.8 x 21 (32³⁄₁₆ x 8¼)
Mike and Annie Belkin Collection

José Chardiet (American, b. Cuba, 1956)
Untitled, 1992
Blown glass and enamel; 44.1 x 31.2 (17⅜ x 12¼)
Mike and Annie Belkin Collection

Dale Chihuly (American, b. 1941)
Blanket Series, Untitled, 1976
Blown glass; 29 x 18.7 (11⅜ x 7⁵⁄₁₆)
Heinz and Elizabeth Wolf Collection

Dale Chihuly (American, b. 1941)
Blanket Series, Untitled, 1976
Blown glass; 27.9 x 14.3 (11 x 5⅝)
Heinz and Elizabeth Wolf Collection

Dale Chihuly (American, b. 1941)
Cadmium Yellow Persian Set, 1990
Blown glass; 21.9 x 47.9 x 24.4 (8⅝ x 18¹³⁄₁₆ x 9⁹⁄₁₆)
The Cleveland Museum of Art, The Mary Spedding
Milliken Memorial Collection, Gift of William
Mathewson Milliken 1991.76

Dale Chihuly (American, b. 1941)
Cobalt Green and Violet Wall Piece, 1990
Blown glass; 91.4 x 152.4 x 45.8 (36 x 60 x 18)
Collection of Alan Markowitz, M.D., and Cathy Pollard

Dale Chihuly (American, b. 1941)
Early White Seaform Set, 1981
Blown glass; 18.2 x 47.3 (7⅛ x 18⅝)
Francine and Benson Pilloff Collection

Dale Chihuly (American, b. 1941)
Gilded Blue Tortoise Shell Float, 1992
Blown glass; 57.1 x 66.5 (22½ x 26³⁄₁₆)
Francine and Benson Pilloff Collection

Dale Chihuly (American, b. 1941)
Gilded Yellow Venetian with Lilies, 1991
Blown glass; 52.5 x 57 (20⅝ x 22⁷⁄₁₆)
Francine and Benson Pilloff Collection

Dale Chihuly (American, b. 1941)
Gold over Cobalt Blue Venetian with One Coil, 1991
Blown glass; 78.4 x 33 (30⅞ x 13)
Francine and Benson Pilloff Collection

Dale Chihuly (American, b. 1941)
Gray Seaform Macchia Set with Black Lip Wrap, 1983
Blown glass; 16.7 x 51.1 (6⁹⁄₁₆ x 20⅛)
Francine and Benson Pilloff Collection

Dale Chihuly (American, b. 1941)
Green and Magenta Chandelier, 1995
Blown glass; 61 x 76.2 x 76.2 (24 x 30 x 30)
Francine and Benson Pilloff Collection

Dale Chihuly (American, b. 1941)
Green and Oxblood Ikebana with Two Red Flowers, 1992
Blown glass; 154.9 x 99 x 43.2 (61 x 39 x 17)
Francine and Benson Pilloff Collection

Dale Chihuly (American, b. 1941)
Lavender Persian Set, 1988
Blown glass; 21 x 57.5 (8¼ x 22⅝)
Lorrie and Alvin Magid Collection

Dale Chihuly (American, b. 1941)
Macchia, 1988
Blown glass; 41.6 x 81.8 (16⅜ x 32³⁄₁₆)
Francine and Benson Pilloff Collection

Dale Chihuly (American, b. 1941)
Periwinkle Blue Macchia with Black Lip Wrap, 1995
Blown glass; 29 x 40.5 (11⅜ x 15¹⁵⁄₁₆)
Dan and Linda Rocker Silverberg Collection

Dale Chihuly (American, b. 1941)
Pink Seaform with Black Lip Wraps, 1991
Blown glass; 34.3 x 53.3 x 45.7 (13½ x 21 x 18)
Mike and Annie Belkin Collection

Dale Chihuly (American, b. 1941)
Silver over Rose Madder Drawing Float, 1992
Blown glass; 55.9 x 45.8 x 55.9 (22 x 18 x 22)
Collection of Mr. and Mrs. Charles Debordeau

Dale Chihuly (American, b. 1941)
Translucent White Basket Set with Black Lip Wraps, 1992
Blown glass; 45.2 x 57.2 (17¾ x 22½)
Francine and Benson Pilloff Collection

Daniel Clayman (American, b. 1957)
Untitled, 1990
Cast glass and patinated copper; 55.9 x 36.3 (22 x 14¼)
Mike and Annie Belkin Collection

Henri Cros (French, 1840–1907)
Incantation, 1892
Pâte-de-verre; 33.4 x 23.3 (13⅛ x 9⅛)
The Cleveland Museum of Art, James Parmelee Fund
1969.24

Dan Dailey (American, b. 1947)
Buzz, 1990
Blown glass; 28.8 x 54 (11⁵⁄₁₆ x 21¼)
Clarine and Harvey Saks Collection

Dan Dailey (American, b. 1947)
Jazz Man, 1988
Blown glass with enamel decoration; 39.2 x 27
(15⁷⁄₁₆ x 10⅝)
Francine and Benson Pilloff Collection

Dan Dailey (American, b. 1947)
Les Danseurs, 1979
Pâte-de-verre; 36 x 35.8 (14⅛ x 14¹⁄₁₆)
Francine and Benson Pilloff Collection

François-Émile Décorchemont (French, 1880–1971)
Vase, about 1922
Pâte-de-verre; h. 10 (3¹⁵⁄₁₆), diam. 11.6 (4⁹⁄₁₆)
The Cleveland Museum of Art, Gift of Louise Rorimer
Dushkin 1983.210

Fritz Dreisbach (American, b. 1941)
Vase, 1986
Blown glass; 24.4 x 19.7 (9⁹⁄₁₆ x 7¾)
Mike and Annie Belkin Collection

Edris Eckhardt (American, b. 1907)
Cherubim, 1955
Cast glass; 15 x 22.1 (5⅞ x 8¹¹⁄₁₆)
The Cleveland Museum of Art, Gift of The Cleveland
Art Association 1956.92

Edris Eckhardt (American, b. 1907)
Horse, 1976
Cast glass; 20 x 13.8 x 8.1 (7⅞ x 5½ x 3¼)
The Cleveland Museum of Art, Gift of Mr. and Mrs.
Samuel H. Lamport 1994.217

Edris Eckhardt (American, b. 1907)
In the Garden of the Sea (Neither Night Nor Day), 1979
Laminated glass; 29.5 x 10.7 (11⅝ x 4¼)
Heinz and Elizabeth Wolf Collection

Edris Eckhardt (American, b. 1907)
Untitled, 1969
Cast glass; 31 x 21.2 (12³⁄₁₆ x 8⁵⁄₁₆)
Ralph and Terry Kovel Collection

Edris Eckhardt (American, b. 1907)
Wonder, 1982
Cast bronze and glass; h. 41.5 (16⁵⁄₁₆), with base
52.4 x 9 (20⅝ x 3½)
Heinz and Elizabeth Wolf Collection

Michael M. Glancy (American, b. 1950)
Convoluted Continuum, 1986
Blown and sandblasted glass with copper electroplate;
14.1 x 12.2 (5½ x 4¾)
Mike and Annie Belkin Collection

Robin Grebe (American, b. 1957)
The Cultivation, 1993
Cast glass and metal; 132 x 17.8 (52 x 7)
Dan and Linda Rocker Silverberg Collection

Henry Halem (American, b. 1938)
Baby Doll, 1976
Cast glass; 31.1 x 33.4 x 8.3 (12¼ x 13⅛ x 3¼)
Mike and Annie Belkin Collection

Henry Halem (American, b. 1938)
Black Nude, 1984
Vitrolite with painted enamel; 61 x 61 (24 x 24)
Mike and Annie Belkin Collection

Henry Halem (American, b. 1938)
Bowl, 1977
Blown glass; h. 14.7 (5¾), diam. 15.9 (6¼)
The Cleveland Museum of Art, Gift of Mr. and Mrs.
Samuel H. Lamport 1994.214

Henry Halem (American, b. 1938)
Constructivist Construction, 1986
Glass (with plastic?); 104.6 x 80.5 (41³/₁₆ x 31¹¹/₁₆)
Heinz and Elizabeth Wolf Collection

Henry Halem (American, b. 1938)
Figure #1, 1988
Vitrolite with painted enamel; 64.8 x 48.3 x 8.9
(25½ x 19 x 3½)
Mike and Annie Belkin Collection

David R. Huchthausen (American, b. 1951)
Leitungs Scherbe, 1986
Laminated, cut, and polished glass; 32.4 x 50.2
(12¾ x 19¾)
Jules and Fran Belkin Collection

Jack Ink (American, b. 1944)
Landscape 1075, 1983
Cast glass; 19.7 x 15.6 x 3.9 (7¾ x 6⅛ x 1½)
The Cleveland Museum of Art, The Harold T. Clark
Educational Extension Fund 1984.1128

Jack Ink (American, b. 1944)
Untitled, 1987
Mold-blown glass with metal frame; 10.6 x 21.1
(4⅛ x 8⁵/₁₆)
Heinz and Elizabeth Wolf Collection

Judy Jensen (American, b. 1953)
On the Road, 1993
Reverse painting on glass; 85.7 x 81.6 (33¾ x 32⅛)
Francine and Benson Pilloff Collection

Kreg Kallenberger (American, b. 1950)
Cuneiform Series, 1986
Blown, cut, and polished glass; 17.4 x 18.6
(6¹³/₁₆ x 7⁵/₁₆)
Mike and Annie Belkin Collection

Jon Kuhn (American, b. 1949)
143 Linda, 1993
Laminated, cut, and polished glass; 25.4 x 25.4 x 25.4
(10 x 10 x 10)
Dan and Linda Rocker Silverberg Collection

Jon Kuhn (American, b. 1949)
Clear Skies, 1993
Laminated, cut, and polished glass; 76.2 x 76.2 (30 x 30)
Ester Goldsmith Collection

Dominick Labino (American, 1910–1987)
Emergence, 1969
Blown glass; 26.1 x 9.7 x 8 (10¼ x 3¹³/₁₆ x 3³/₁₆)
The Cleveland Museum of Art, Gift of Mr. and Mrs.
Samuel H. Lamport 1994.215

Dominick Labino (American, 1910–1987)
Faceted Fountain, 1978
Blown glass; 17.2 x 14.3 x 9.7 (6¾ x 5⅝ x 3¹³/₁₆)
The Cleveland Museum of Art, Gift of Mr. and Mrs.
James A. Saks 1980.124

Dominick Labino (American, 1910–1987)
Iceberg, 1965
Blown glass; h. 21.6 (8½)
The Cleveland Museum of Art, Gift of the artist
1967.161

Dominick Labino (American, 1910–1987)
Long-Chain Molecules, 1973
Cast glass; 200.6 x 45.7 x 1.8 (79 x 18 x ¹¹/₁₆),
201.4 x 45.7 x 1.9 (79⁵/₁₆ x 18 x ¾)
The Cleveland Museum of Art, Gift of Carol and
Franklin Milgrim in honor of Berenice Kent 1991.31,
1991.32

Dominick Labino (American, 1910–1987)
Untitled, 1970
Blown glass; 26 x 13.3 (10³/₁₆ x 5³/₁₆)
Collection of Mr. and Mrs. James A. Saks

Dominick Labino (American, 1910–1987)
Vase, 1965
Blown glass; 25.8 x 16.8 (10⅛ x 6¹¹/₁₆)
The Cleveland Museum of Art, Gift of the artist
1967.162

John Lewis (American, b. 1942)
Zig Zag Micro Pedestal, 1991
Cast glass; 85.1 x 24.2 (33½ x 9½)
Ann and Robert Friedman Collection

Marvin Lipofsky (American, b. 1938)
California Color Series 1986–87 #16, 1986–87
Blown glass; 27.3 x 34.2 (10¾ x 13⁷/₁₆)
Clarine and Harvey Saks Collection

Harvey K. Littleton (American, b. 1922)
Descending Arch, 1988
Blown glass; part 1: 16.7 x 11.3 (6⁹/₁₆ x 4⁷/₁₆),
part 2: 36.8 x 25.9 (14⁷/₁₆ x 10³/₁₆)
Clarine and Harvey Saks Collection

Harvey K. Littleton (American, b. 1922)
Descending Sliced Arches, 1984
Blown glass; part 1: 20.4 x 15.3 x 5.2 (8 x 6 x 2), part 2:
38.2 x 15.3 x 28 (15 x 6 x 11), part 3: 38.2 x 15.3 x 28 (15
x 6 x 11), part 4: 20.4 x 15.3 x 5.2 (8 x 6 x 2)
Collection of Alan Markowitz, M.D., and Cathy Pollard

Harvey K. Littleton (American, b. 1922)
Purple Conical Intersection, 1985
Blown glass; 24.2 x 24.1 (9½ x 9⁷/₁₆)
Helen and David Kangesser Collection

Harvey K. Littleton (American, b. 1922)
Standing Mobile Arc, 1989
Blown glass; part 1: 12.5 x 12.9 (4⅞ x 5¹/₁₆),
part 2: 49.1 x 38.2 (19⁵/₁₆ x 15)
Lorrie and Alvin Magid Collection

Flora C. Mace (American, b. 1949)
Joey Kirkpatrick (American, b. 1952)
Cloaked Doll, 1983
Blown glass and wood; 34.4 x 9.4 (13½ x 3¹¹/₁₆)
Francine and Benson Pilloff Collection

Flora C. Mace (American, b. 1949)
Joey Kirkpatrick (American, b. 1952)
Pear, 1992
Blown glass; 58.5 x 38.8 (23 x 15¼)
Francine and Benson Pilloff Collection

Flora C. Mace (American, b. 1949)
Joey Kirkpatrick (American, b. 1952)
Seasonal Sphire, 1994
Blown glass and wood; 208.2 x 116.8 x 58.4
(82 x 46 x 23)
Francine and Benson Pilloff Collection

Flora C. Mace (American, b. 1949)
Joey Kirkpatrick (American, b. 1952)
Untitled (Bowl with Birds), 1983
Blown glass and wire drawings; 16.6 x 19.8
(6½ x 7¾)
Francine and Benson Pilloff Collection

Maurice Marinot (French, 1882–1960)
Blue-Green Bottle, about 1924–25
Blown glass, acid etched; 16.8 x 10.4 (6⁹⁄₁₆ x 4¹⁄₁₆)
The Cleveland Museum of Art, Dudley P. Allen Fund
1938.382

Maurice Marinot (French, 1882–1960)
Vase, 1928
Blown glass, acid etched; h. 22 (8⅝), diam. 16.6 (6½)
The Cleveland Museum of Art, Gift of C. M. de Hauke
1929.114

Dante Marioni (American, b. 1964)
Giant Whopper Vase, 1992
Blown glass; 111.8 x 36.2 (44 x 14¼)
Francine and Benson Pilloff Collection

Dante Marioni (American, b. 1964)
Ivory and Black, 1996
Blown glass; part 1: 67.3 x 22 x 15.9 (26½ x 8⅝ x 6¼),
part 2: 76.8 x 17.2 x 15.9 (30¼ x 6¾ x 6¼), part 3: 37.5
x 38.5 x 27.3 (14¾ x 15⅛ x 10¾)
Mike and Annie Belkin Collection

Dante Marioni (American, b. 1964)
Red Leaf, about 1995
Blown glass; 85.8 x 18.8 (33¾ x 7⅜)
Private collection

Sherry Markovitz (American, b. 1947)
Swoosh, 1991
Mixed media with beads, papier-mâché, and fiberglass;
238.6 x 12.7 x 22.9 (94 x 5 x 9)
Francine and Benson Pilloff Collection

Richard Marquis (American, b. 1945)
Teapot Trophy, 1989
Blown glass; 80.3 x 26.7 (31⅝ x 10½)
Mike and Annie Belkin Collection

Earl McCutchen (American, 1918–1985)
Plate, 1960
Slumped glass; 1.4 x 17.2 x 17.2 (½ x 6¾ x 6¾)
The Cleveland Museum of Art, Anonymous Gift
1960.263

William R. McKinney (American, b. 1958)
20th-Century Primitive, 1987
Cast glass; 26.1 x 10.8 x 12 (10¼ x 4¼ x 4¹¹⁄₁₆)
The Cleveland Museum of Art, The Harold T. Clark
Educational Extension Fund 1987.1008

William R. McKinney (American, b. 1958)
Bill's Ball, 1986
Blown glass; 12.2 x 12.2 x 9 (4¾ x 4¾ x 3½)
The Cleveland Museum of Art, The Harold T. Clark
Educational Extension Fund 1987.1009

William Morris (American, b. 1957)
Burial Urn with Tool, 1991
Blown and cast glass; 51.4 x 57.8 (20¼ x 22¾)
Francine and Benson Pilloff Collection

William Morris (American, b. 1957)
Canopic Jar—Mountain Lion, about 1995
Blown and cast glass; 63.2 x 22.3 (24⅞ x 8¾)
Private collection

William Morris (American, b. 1957)
Petroglyph Vessel, 1989
Blown glass; 55.5 x 50.1 (21¹³⁄₁₆ x 19¹¹⁄₁₆)
Clarine and Harvey Saks Collection

William Morris (American, b. 1957)
Rhyton Bull, 1996
Blown and manipulated glass; 17.8 x 26 (7 x 10³⁄₁₆)
Ann and Robert Friedman Collection

William Morris (American, b. 1957)
Standing Stone, 1989
Mold-blown glass; 118.1 x 28 (46½ x 11)
Francine and Benson Pilloff Collection

Jay Musler (American, b. 1949)
Ugly Bowl, 1989
Slumped glass, plate-glass mosaic, and applied oil
pigments; h. 41.3 (16¼), diam. 54.6 (21½)
Mike and Annie Belkin Collection

Joel Philip Myers (American, b. 1934)
Arctic Landscape II, 1990
Blown glass; 38.2 x 45 (15 x 17¹¹⁄₁₆)
Private collection

Joel Philip Myers (American, b. 1934)
Arctic Sky II, 1991
Blown glass; 22.2 x 73.8 (8¾ x 29¹⁄₁₆)
Helen and David Kangesser Collection

Joel Philip Myers (American, b. 1934)
Contiguous Fragment Series, 1981
Blown glass, acid etched, and applied glass elements;
31.8 x 11.2 (12½ x 4⅜)
Mike and Annie Belkin Collection

Henri Navarre (French, 1885–1971)
Vase, about 1930–35
Blown glass; h. 22.5 (8¹³⁄₁₆), diam. 14.6 (5¾)
The Cleveland Museum of Art, The A. W. Ellenberger
Sr. Endowment Fund 1977.12

Robert Clark Palusky (American, b. 1942)
Figure Standing on Dice, 1989
Mold-blown, cut, ground, and polished glass; 72.4 x 21.5
(28½ x 8⁷⁄₁₆)
Jules and Fran Belkin Collection

Thomas Patti (American, b. 1943)
Compacted Blue with Green, 1986
Fused, hand-shaped, ground, and polished glass; 9.5 x
13.6 (3¾ x 5⁵⁄₁₆)
Private collection, Cleveland

Michael Pavlik (American, b. Czechoslovakia, 1941)
Kunsterstruction, 1993
Cut and polished glass; 81.3 x 45.8 x 45.8 (32 x 18 x 18)
Dan and Linda Rocker Silverberg Collection

Michael Pavlik (American, b. Czechoslovakia, 1941)
Whirling Red Triangles, 1994
Cut and polished glass; 38.1 x 40.7 x 30.6 (15 x 16 x 12)
Dan and Linda Rocker Silverberg Collection

Mark Peiser (American, b. 1938)
Ascension Series, 1986
Cast glass, cut and polished; 35.6 x 17.2 x 7.6
(14 x 6¾ x 3)
Mike and Annie Belkin Collection

Mark Peiser (American, b. 1938)
Escher's Tower, 1986
Cast glass, cut and polished; 35.9 x 20 (14⅛ x 7⅞)
Mike and Annie Belkin Collection

Mark Peiser (American, b. 1938)
Leaning Moon, 1985
Cast glass, cut and polished; 23.3 x 20 (9⅛ x 7⅞)
Helen and David Kangesser Collection

Mark Peiser (American, b. 1938)
Mountain Skyscape, 1993
Cast glass, cut and polished; 21.5 x 43.1 (8⁷⁄₁₆ x 16¹⁵⁄₁₆)
Ann and Robert Friedman Collection

Stephen Powell (American, b. 1951)
Pregnant Bust Jones, about 1995
Blown glass; 84.9 x 47 (33⁷⁄₁₆ x 18½)
Private collection

Christopher Ries (American, b. 1952)
Satin Pleats
Cut and polished glass; 44.5 x 24.8 (17½ x 9¾)
Private collection

Richard Q. Ritter Jr. (American, b. 1940)
Bowl, 1975
Blown glass; h. 15 (5⅞), diam. 16.4 (6½)
The Cleveland Museum of Art, Gift of Mr. and Mrs.
Samuel H. Lamport 1994.216

Richard Q. Ritter Jr. (American, b. 1940)
Large Bowl, 1994
Blown glass with inclusions; h. 13.2 (5³⁄₁₆),
diam. 30.6 (12)
Ann and Robert Friedman Collection

Sally Rogers (American, b. 1960)
Moraine, 1992
Mold-blown glass; part 1: 37.7 x 18.5 (14¹³⁄₁₆ x 7¼),
part 2: 39.3 x 18.2 (15⁷⁄₁₆ x 7⅛), part 3: 38 x 19.6
(14¹⁵⁄₁₆ x 7¹¹⁄₁₆)
Private collection

Daniel Rothenfeld (American, b. 1953)
Chrysalis, 1983
Laminated plate glass; 58.3 x 19.8 (22¹⁵⁄₁₆ x 7¾)
Dan and Linda Rocker Silverberg Collection

Ginny Ruffner (American, b. 1952)
Jewels of Spring, 1991
Lamp-worked glass and paint; 44.7 x 42.6 (17⁹⁄₁₆ x 16¾)
Helen and David Kangesser Collection

Ginny Ruffner (American, b. 1952)
Tunnel of Love Wears Heartbreak Pajamas, 1989
Lamp-worked glass and paint; 30.3 x 63.2 (11¹⁵⁄₁₆ x 24⅞)
Francine and Benson Pilloff Collection

Kari Russell-Pool (American, b. 1967)
Marc Petrovic (American, b. 1967)
Flush, 1995
Lamp-worked and blown glass; 49.2 x 35.6 x 20.3
(19⅜ x 14 x 8)
Lorrie and Alvin Magid Collection

Italo Scanga (American, b. Italy, 1932)
Endangered Species Series: Spotted Owl, 1993
Blown glass and painted metal; 87 x 30.9 (34¼ x 12⅛)
Ann and Robert Friedman Collection

Judith Schaechter (American, b. 1961)
Death in the Flesh, 1989
Stained glass; 44.1 x 76.9 (17⅜ x 30¼)
Francine and Benson Pilloff Collection

Joyce Scott (American, b. 1948)
Flaming Skeleton Series #1, 1993
Mixed media and glass beads; 33.6 x 28.4 (13³⁄₁₆ x 11³⁄₁₆)
Francine and Benson Pilloff Collection

Joyce Scott (American, b. 1948)
Holocaust, 1994
Mixed media and glass beads; 39.7 x 30.5 (15⅝ x 12)
Francine and Benson Pilloff Collection

Joyce Scott (American, b. 1948)
Night and Crystal, 1993
Mixed media and glass beads; 36.7 x 26.7 (14⁷⁄₁₆ x 10½)
Francine and Benson Pilloff Collection

Paul Seide (American, b. 1949)
Radio Lights, 1986
Radioactivated neon; part 1: 52.7 x 26 (20¾ x 10³⁄₁₆), part
2: 32.1 x 21 (12⅝ x 8¼)
Mike and Annie Belkin Collection

Mary Shaffer (American, b. 1947)
Inverted Cube, 1991
Bronze and slumped glass; part 1: 98.5 x 31.1 (38¾ x
12¼); part 2: 97.2 x 34.4 (38¼ x 13½)
Helen and David Kangesser Collection

Mary Kay Simoni (American, b. 1955)
(W)Hole TV Window, 1996
Laminated glass; 32 x 31.7 (12⁹⁄₁₆ x 12⁷⁄₁₆)
Dan and Linda Rocker Silverberg Collection

Mary Kay Simoni (American, b. 1955)
No Mo, 1989
Laminated glass with plastic additions; 52.9 x 25.6
(20¹³⁄₁₆ x 10¹⁄₁₆)
Heinz and Elizabeth Wolf Collection

Paul J. Stankard (American, b. 1943)
Allium, 1989
Lamp-worked and encased glass; 12.7 x 7.3 x 7
(5 x 2⅞ x 2¾)
The Cleveland Museum of Art, Seventy-fifth anniversary
gift of the George M. Foley Family 1991.131

Paul J. Stankard (American, b. 1943)
Cactus Botanical, 1990
Lamp-worked and encased glass; 15.2 x 7.6 x 7.6
(6 x 3 x 3)
Mike and Annie Belkin Collection

Paul J. Stankard (American, b. 1943)
Cloistered Indian Pipes Botanical, 1989
Lamp-worked and encased glass; 15.5 x 7.1 (6¹⁄₁₆ x 2¾)
Mike and Annie Belkin Collection

Paul J. Stankard (American, b. 1943)
Coronet Botanical with Insects, 1995
Lamp-worked and encased glass; 11.9 x 7.2 (4¹¹⁄₁₆ x 2¹³⁄₁₆)
Mike and Annie Belkin Collection

Paul J. Stankard (American, b. 1943)
Mountain Laurel Botanical, 1994
Lamp-worked and encased glass; 12.7 x 8 x 7
(5 x 3⅛ x 2¾)
Mike and Annie Belkin Collection

Paul J. Stankard (American, b. 1943)
Paphiopedium with Spirit, 1991
Lamp-worked and encased glass; h. 5.3 (2¹⁄₁₆),
diam. 8 (3⅛)
Virginia Q. Foley Collection

Paul J. Stankard (American, b. 1943)
Water Lily Environment with Spirits, 1987
Lamp-worked and encased glass; h. 5 (1¹⁵⁄₁₆),
diam. 8.4 (3¼)
Virginia Q. Foley Collection

Paul J. Stankard (American, b. 1943)
Rick Ayotte (American, b. 1944)
Environmental with Turtle, 1995
Lamp-worked and encased glass; 5.6 x 8.4 (2³⁄₁₆ x 3¼)
Mike and Annie Belkin Collection

Therman Statom (American, b. 1953)
Ocean Travel, 1993
Painted glass and mixed media; 139.6 x 106.7 x 81.3
(55 x 42 x 32)
Dan and Linda Rocker Silverberg Collection

Mark Sudduth (American, b. 1960)
Inside-Out II, 1986
Cast glass; 27.3 x 14.7 x 9.6 (10¾ x 5¾ x 3¾)
The Cleveland Museum of Art, The Sarah Stern Michael
Fund 1987.68

Steve Tobin (American, b. 1957)
Doorway, 1992
Sand-cast glass with injected hot inclusions, polished;
41.5 x 43 (16⁵⁄₁₆ x 16¹⁵⁄₁₆)
Ann and Robert Friedman Collection

Karla Trinkley (American, b. 1956)
Pinky, 1994
Pâte-de-verre; h. 30 (11¹³⁄₁₆), diam. 51.9 (20⁷⁄₁₆)
Mike and Annie Belkin Collection

Karla Trinkley (American, b. 1956)
Untitled, 1986
Pâte-de-verre; h. 29.9 (11¾), diam. 31.8 (12½)
Mike and Annie Belkin Collection

Mark Vance (American, b. 1947)
Vase, 1977
Blown glass; h. 16.5 (6½), diam. 16.5 (6½)
The Cleveland Museum of Art, Gift of George and Lois
Vance 1996.263

Janusz Walentynowicz (American, b. Poland, 1956)
The Bundle, 1994 or 1995
Cast glass and paint; 50 x 39.8 (19¹¹⁄₁₆ x 15⅝)
Ann and Robert Friedman Collection

Steven Weinberg (American, b. 1954)
Untitled, 1984
Cast glass, polished; 12.9 x 21.7 (5¹⁄₁₆ x 8½)
Mike and Annie Belkin Collection

Steven Weinberg (American, b. 1954)
Untitled, 1988
Cast glass, polished; 20.9 x 20.9 (8³⁄₁₆ x 8³⁄₁₆)
Clarine and Harvey Saks Collection

Steven Weinberg (American, b. 1954)
Untitled, 1991
Cast glass, polished; 23.5 x 22.5 x 22.5 (9¼ x 8¹³⁄₁₆ x 8¹³⁄₁₆)
The Cleveland Museum of Art, Seventy-fifth anniversary
gift of Annie and Mike Belkin 1992.101

Brent Kee Young (American, b. 1946)
Fossil Fantasy: Fishin' with Bill, 1978
Blown glass; h. 13.7 (5⅜), diam. 11.4 (4½)
The Cleveland Museum of Art, The Harold T. Clark
Educational Extension Fund 1978.1025

Brent Kee Young (American, b. 1946)
Untitled, 1977
Blown glass; 23.7 x 13.9 (9⁵⁄₁₆ x 5⁷⁄₁₆)
Heinz and Elizabeth Wolf Collection

Brent Kee Young (American, b. 1946)
Vase, 1982
Mold-blown glass; 20.3 x 21 x 19 (8 x 8¼ x 7½)
The Cleveland Museum of Art, Louis D. Kacalieff,
M.D., Fund 1982.60

Toots Zynsky (American, b. 1951)
Angry Birds from the Birds of Paradise Series, 1987
Pulled and fused glass threads; 13.7 x 29.5 (5⅜ x 11⁹⁄₁₆)
Mike and Annie Belkin Collection

Toots Zynsky (American, b. 1951)
Italian Chaos IV
Pulled and fused glass threads; 19.4 x 38.1 (7⅝ x 15)
Private collection

Toots Zynsky (American, b. 1951)
Paris Chaos, 1994
Pulled and fused glass threads; 15.6 x 38.2 (6⅛ x 15)
Ann and Robert Friedman Collection

Index of Artists

First published in the United States in 1997 on the occasion of the exhibition *Glass Today: American Studio Glass from Cleveland Collections,* 22 June–14 September 1997.

Distributed by the University of Washington Press, Seattle.

Dimensions, as supplied by lenders, are give in centimeters (and inches), height by width by depth or height by diameter. Works are arranged chronologically in the artist's oeuvre within the catalogue of the exhibition and alphabetically by artist and title in the checklist.

Cover: Joel Philip Myers, *Arctic Sky II,* 1991 (detail). Helen and David Kangesser Collection.

Library of Congress Cataloging-in-Publication Data
Hawley, Henry H.
  Glass today : American studio glass from Cleveland collections / Henry H. Hawley.
    p.   cm.
  Catalogue of an exhibition with the same title organized by the Cleveland Museum of Art, June 22–Sept. 14, 1997.
    Includes index.
    ISBN 0-940717-41-7 (paper : alk. paper)
    1. Art glass—United States—History—20th century—Exhibitions. 2. Art glass—Private collections—Ohio—Cleveland—Exhibitions. I. Cleveland Museum of Art.   II. Title.
NK5439.A77H38   1997
748.2913—dc21   97-18605
                                             CIP

Editor: Barbara J. Bradley
Designer: Laurence Channing
Production Manager: Charles Szabla
Printing: Great Lakes Lithograph Company
Photography: All photographs of works of art were taken by Howard Agriesti, museum photographer, except those on pages 36 (top left), 47 (top), 53 (top), 54 (top), 77, 80 (taken by Ric Murray), 93 (bottom), 94 (bottom), 95, (top), and 105 (top).

ISBN: 0-940717-41-7